MY GAY CHURCH DAYS

with much ♡

GEORGE AZAR

MY GAY
CHURCH DAYS

MEMOIR OF A CLOSETED
EVANGELICAL PASTOR
WHO EVENTUALLY HAD
ENOUGH

Roman Matthews Publishing Company

DEDICATION & RECOGNITION

This book is dedicated first and foremost to my sister and brother. Without your love and support, I wouldn't be me.

To my Christian friends: Scarlette, Liam, and Emma – for being clear examples of what it means to be Christians living your faith with conviction and sincerity.

To Dr. Rachael – a world of thanks for your professional help, support, and never giving up on me.

To my dear friends – for your unwavering love.

A percentage of the proceeds from the purchase of this book will be donated to The Trevor Project, a national 24-hour, toll-free confidential suicide hotline for LGBTQ youth.

Consider it a tithe.

CONTENTS

CONTENTS

CONTENTS

5

Resurrection

MY GAY CHURCH DAYS

Memoir of a closeted evangelical pastor who eventually had enough.

A SPECIAL NOTE TO MY EVANGELICAL READERS

There are *definitely* some things in this book that will offend you or cause you to be angry. I know I would be offended if I were still in the faith. All I ask is that you read with an open heart to hear someone else's experience and perspective. I understand that this can be a complicated story to read as I will be sharing thoughts that differ from your own and strike to the core of your faith. Please keep in mind: to your community, my words may be offensive, but to my community, your words can literally mean the loss of someone's life. Real humans have taken their own lives to rid themselves of their "sinfulness." Their rejection turned to pain, torment, self-hatred, depression, and sometimes death. Many may view their experience on earth as too unbearable or believe that they are a dirty, rotten sinner needing a savior. Some may feel so unlovable to the point they'd instead rid themselves from this earth than have to experience their traumas propagated by the Evangelical belief system. Please be warned: this book is not for the faint of heart.

IN THE BEGINNING

I was constantly told, "Your testimony is the only thing they can't refute." It was the backbone of the entire faith. You could debate semantics about the faith until you were blue in the face, but the one thing nobody could take away from you was your testimony. Your testimony is your story about how "God" moved in your life to draw you to "Him." How nobody could take away your experience because it was yours alone.

One of the most powerful statements made to me during my departure from the church came from the senior pastor. After I laid out my grievances and petitioned for my departure, the tension in the room was alleviated by one of the most significant things he ever said to me: "No matter where you are or what you do, God is going to use you in miraculous ways for His glory." I didn't feel the total weight of his words until later in life – long after I left the faith. Little did I know how right he was going to be.

When I first moved to Los Angeles, I found myself in an emergency room after passing out from what I thought was a heart attack. Test results revealed that my heart was healthy but under constant pressure due to my mental health. I had worked myself into a major panic attack that caused me to feel a sharp pain in my left arm that caused me to pass out while driving. I discovered that day that a severe panic attack could resemble a heart attack. I knew the source of this anxiety: I was contending with relationship issues with my first boyfriend, and I had just moved to a new city where I had no friends to fall back on. Most of my social life had been rooted in the church.

I knew I needed help.

After getting on an SSRI to regulate my anxiety and depression, I somewhat regained my stride. I felt better about myself, and the night terrors became less frequent. What always seemed to linger, though, was the guilt of living my gay life. I clung to deep-seated beliefs about God, heaven, sin, and hell that caused me to doubt my pursuit of happiness. I was faced with a choice between my faith and being my true self.

After years of therapy, professional ups and downs, love gained and lost, I decided to choose myself.

As of this writing, I'm about seven years removed from my faith, but the remnants of my past remain. Unfortunately, neurological pathways are a tricky bunch to retrain, and to this day, I battle with the thoughts about myself that are flat-out lies: I'm a horrible sinner, and I was never worthy of true love.

Although I no longer ascribe to the Christian faith, its influence has left an everlasting impact on my life. Learning to love myself, accept myself, and belong to myself has been one of the most challenging yet most rewarding ventures of my life.

The year 2020 brought about a massive shift in my life. Like many, the Covid-19 pandemic changed so much for me. Before the world stopped, I was working at a public accounting firm, and the first deadline to submit extensions for our clients' tax returns was approaching. I was pulling long hours in the office and going through the motions of the busy season. At times I found myself going to Starbucks and staring at the baristas in envy. I was jealous that they could leave their work at work, jealous that they had set hours for their shifts. I was quickly losing patience with not only my job but my career path.

When the pandemic required us to work from home for the unforeseeable future, I was actually filled with excitement, unlike most other people. I felt like I had a new lease on life; the air felt electric! I started working out at home, signed up for different fitness memberships and YouTube video demonstrations, learned how to play the piano. I even attempted to learn a new language!

Eventually, however, the weight of the pandemic and this new abnormal set in. I realized that even before this significant disruption, I had filled my days with different distractions. It dawned on me that something as simple as driving to work had even become one. Now, I was doing precisely that in quarantine: distracting myself.

After a few months, I began facing some of my greatest enemies more intensely than usual: self-loathing, body dysmorphia, internalized homophobia, and fears of being alone. I started to rely on a former addiction: opioids.

I tapped into the reserve I stashed away over the years from former surgeries (I didn't mind the expiration dates), trying to numb the pain of losing my mom earlier that year to her plethora of years-long painful chronic illnesses. I wrestled with the complicated relationship we had and the thoughts of our last moments together. I was also trying to feel something, anything, after being numb to the cares of the world. I would pop a couple of pills and drive to the beach to disconnect from my phone and the rabbit holes I would find myself down.

No longer was I able to distract myself by making plans or running off to work. The world stood still as we processed uncertainty around when the endless stay-at-home orders would lift. *How long would we be stuck at home? How much longer will I be alone?* Isolation began to kick in, and it was coming for blood.

After consulting with my therapist and psychiatrist to get myself back on healthier alternatives to hallucinatory drugs (getting back on an SSRI), I was finally forced to face the one person I'd been running from my entire life: myself. I sat with myself in my Los Angeles apartment, learning who I was and what I liked, what my deepest fears were, what I found attractive or repulsive. I was forced to discover who I was and how I ticked. I analyzed my thoughts, realizing that antiquated belief systems still propped up many of my beliefs about myself in Christianity.

These were belief systems once used to justify why I wasn't acting upon my homosexuality. Belief systems that told me I was disgusting and needed saving, that my friends, family, and very good people were going to hell because they didn't say a specific prayer or believe the man in the sky was their true lord and savior. Belief systems that would kick me down to hell should I become a wayward sheep.

I no longer identified with these belief systems. However, they still influenced my image: I was unworthy of true love because I was a disgusting person, and my life would end up with me alone and destined for destruction. These beliefs caused me to look at my body and loathe every aspect of it, and I knew there was unresolved business that needed to be resolved. This book was birthed, going into the depths of my darkest crevices and unearthing the source of my deepest insecurities.

While writing this book, I often dreamt about my time in the church. Sometimes the dreams were pleasant, but mostly they were eerie reminders of painful events. The most revealing was a dream that involved a secret romantic session with Jake, one of my former roommates. I constantly found myself waking up at night, wondering why he was back in my consciousness. I soon realized there was unfinished business there, too – that I needed to get my thoughts and memories out on paper because of how different I am today.

Why Now?

I decided to write this book not out of spite but inspiration. I carried anger and bitterness with me as constant companions for almost two years after leaving the faith – a faith I committed my entire being to for ten years, with most of those years in my youth and early adulthood. I wrote this book to inspire and heal from one of the most peculiar seasons in my life. Not all my experiences were heartbreaking. I experienced moments of great joy and great pain and learned to find meaning through it all.

As a 90's kid with homosexual feelings, I wasn't exposed to positivity and respect towards the homosexual experience. It was still believed that you could "pray the gay away" (like any other sin) or shrink it away through therapy and prescription drugs. The story I lived is the story of so many of those coming to terms with their sexuality and learning to deal with emotional scars that still sting at times. Although my account is unique and unusual – most gay Christian stories end at youth group – I wanted to write this book to let others know you are never a lost cause – even though you may feel lost.

My testimony is one of love earned, community lost, and, eventually, identity found. Regardless of your own story, I hope you can take solace in the essence of my story and experience solidarity in knowing that you are not alone. You *can* choose to find your true self among the voices of others. Perhaps you're currently in the church and have sensed something isn't right. Perhaps you recently left, or perhaps you've never encountered the influence of religion in your life and are looking for a good story. Perhaps you're the parent of a homosexual kid, and you can't seem to wrap your head around the internal struggle they face. Regardless of your motive, I hope that you're able to open your mind to a different perspective and allow in grace and acceptance for those who still may be wandering in the wilderness – especially if that person is you.

Many of the events during my pastoral days were clouded by a sense of fear and anxiety about the person I was hiding. I was afraid of being exposed as a homosexual destined for hell. As a result, I lost myself in the Bayside Church community — a group of people that weren't afraid to take advantage of my vulnerability. I don't blame them for their actions and have since forgiven them; I'm keenly aware that it was my fear in the faith that ultimately allowed me to be manipulated by them. But the image I had of myself was not yet removed from this system of control and self-loathing.

After going through one of the most challenging yet rewarding periods of my life during this dark pandemic quarantine, I was able to apply some new techniques I had learned from therapy, energy work, and journaling. I could now view these events with a sense of healing and fond memories. Events that once brought me down now woke me up from the slumber of my youth; I was ready to denounce harmful beliefs about myself and the world and pursue my true identity. This book is a byproduct of that journaling journey, and I'm excited to share it with you. Hopefully, the journey of *my gay church days* and beyond inspire you to love yourself exactly as you are.

-George Azar

PART

1

YOUNGER YEARS

HOW IT STARTED

I remember my first gay experience. I was in middle school and had made friends with the other geek on campus. Unfortunately, I suffered a double whammy regarding social skills and looks — I was a plump, Middle Eastern boy who loved the Spice Girls and Power Rangers. Posters were plastered over every nook and cranny of the space I called my corner of the bedroom. We lived in a home a postman with three kids could afford — I shared a small space with my older brother, while my sister's "room" was the living room couch.

I didn't have much of a style other than what I thought was trendy or cool. My closet was filled with Hot Topic satirical shirts of famous brands. This was my failed attempt to make light of the dire situation that was my popularity complex. I wanted nothing more than to be a cool

kid, and I thought my "Special K cereal shirt" (which insin-
uated that I was a druggie) would do the trick. Need I say
more?

My insatiable desire to be liked by others manifested
through my identity as our elementary school's loud-
mouthed prankster. I once made a classmate cry when I
screamed at the final number of the countdown to one of
our pop quizzes. I threw her off her game with my loud
shout, and the teacher scolded me. To make matters worse,
the teacher told my mom, who made sure I was repri-
manded for my behavior. I didn't care about the incident;
I'd never liked this girl who everyone seemed to swoon
over. But the wooden stick that became my mom's favorite
form of punishment was waiting for me after school when
I got home. She was a traditional Middle Eastern mother,
raised in a Catholic school and taught by nuns. She took
what she'd learned about child-rearing during her upbringing as her own, which conflicted with my exposure to
American culture. Nevertheless, she did the best with what
she knew.

Being viewed as the "mischievous one" for as long as I
could remember, I played the part until I learned my lesson
in middle school. My antics were quickly squashed as I became the odd man out. Our family lived in county territory
(not big enough to have its own middle or high school), so
my siblings and I were bussed into a larger city. My hometown was barely large enough to have an elementary school

– there were a total of about 50 kids in the entire school, and I was the only boy in my graduating class of 13.

By contrast, my middle school was much bigger, and the kids there had already formed alliances with classmates from the larger elementary schools in the city. So there I was: fat, effeminate, and desperately low on friends; the situation quickly and easily made me the laughingstock of the school.

Strange Alliances

In a desperate attempt to find refuge after being marginalized by my peers, I quickly developed a personality that catered to making friends with adults – teachers, administrative staff, even cafeteria ladies. Before school, on breaks, and during lunch, I often gossiped with the lunch ladies. Yep, this was a glamorous part of my life. It came with great benefits, though, as I became a cookie sampler. After being dropped off in the mornings, I'd dart off to the cafeteria to avoid the bullies, arriving at the reward of being the taste-tester to the first batch of warm cookies and chocolate milk. Consequently, this ritual became a liability to my weight problem.

Middle school was one of the lowest points in my social life. I was so despised that even the math nerds took jabs at me. It felt like I was wearing a target on my forehead. Whether it was due to the way I dressed, the way I conducted myself, or just the fact that I was plump, the torture never seemed to end.

Then I made another strategic alliance: with the middle school kids associated with the local gang. I let them cheat off me during tests in exchange for protection. One day, I was told this punk bully named Roger would kick my ass after class. I told my last-period teacher of this planned attack, as well as one of the gang members. My teacher offered to watch me as I ran to the bus, and Carlos, the member, asked where I had my last class of the day. As the final bell rang, I peeked outside and made a beeline for the bus. I looked back as Roger chased after me, only to be stopped by Carlos and his friends. They held him off for that encounter, but I knew there would be more (especially after enlisting help for this attack). I was in desperate need of saving.

That's when I met my best friend.

Odd Couple

Chris was an intelligent kid with no friends. I don't remember exactly how or when we met, but I do remember our instant connection. He was an extremely talented musician with a sense of confidence that made me jealous. We hung out every day, sometimes at each other's houses, which only intensified the insults and ridicule levied at us. People believed we were gay lovers, and Roger made sure this characterization was broadcast throughout the entire school. It was a form of "popularity" I was not happy about. It got so bad that one day while waiting for the locker rooms to open up so we could get into our PE clothes, the cool kids saw Chris and me walking up and started yelling, "Faggot!" at us.

Chris paid no attention, but I was devastated. I couldn't help but wonder why they were so mean – why did they treat us so poorly? They didn't even know me, so how could they claim to know my sexual identity? This incident eventually led to a physical altercation, as they grabbed Chris and threw him to the ground. The vice-principal (one of the adults with whom I'd formed a friendship) stepped in to break up the incident, pulling the cool kids into her office while she asked us to walk away.

But the attack that day left a permanent scar, and I pondered whether it was wise to be friends with Chris. I enjoyed his company, but the blow of being labeled "gay" was sometimes more than I could handle. I desperately wanted refuge from the bullying, and my allegiance to Chris seemed like a liability.

It wasn't uncommon for me to be made fun of as being gay. My brother, who was two grades above me in school, was the bullies' initial punching bag. He never divulged the cruelty to me – we hated each other too much to be confidants. I just remember being in elementary school and watching him in agony; he'd repeatedly come home with a look of defeat, reeling from how cruel the kids were to him in middle school. I was worried since I was soon to become a member of this school, and I was afraid of what was to come for me.

Just as I feared, I ascended to the throne vacated by my brother. Unfortunately, my inheritance consisted of an insurmountable onslaught of verbal (and sometimes physical) abuse due simply to name recognition. Quite literally, in fact: a version of my last name hyphenated with "gay" at the beginning was the most common term used to describe me.

Enemies From the Start

It didn't help that my brother and I hated each other. I took jabs at him for being gay, and he at me for my weight. We fought incessantly. I once held a knife to him and told him I'd kill him if he ever made fun of me again. (Clearly, that didn't happen – I didn't write this book in prison.)

Quite simply, he and I were like oil and water.

Our younger sister constantly broke up our fights, sometimes by physically separating us. It usually went like this: one of us would make fun of the other, which escalated into hitting; the other hit back, we'd shout insults at each other, my sister would start crying and break us up, and our parents would run into the room. If it were my dad, he'd grab us; if it were my mom, well, her beloved wooden stick was enough to end it. I was too young to understand why my brother and I were such enemies or where our dueling originated. All I knew was that I couldn't tolerate him, and he couldn't tolerate me.

Puberty, along with a suppressed and mysterious sexual appetite, was destructive. Our uncle had given our family a computer, which in those days was a big deal. This was when dial-up and AOL software CDs were a thing. Once online, I watched straight porn and was taken aback because my fantasies involved being the woman in scenarios. This evolved into me drawing pictures of naked men in a secret journal I kept at my grandmother's house (I also kept images I had printed out from straight porn, though I often only looked at the men).

This was my first experience of homosexual feelings, and it felt good. However, I also knew that if I ever were open about that or told anyone, it would *destroy* me at school. So, I knew I had to keep this a secret to the bitter end. Eventually, my secret was revealed thanks to the search history, but I quickly blamed it on my brother. I knew my secret would be the end of me, and I didn't care that he got the blame.

As I got older, I understood why I hated my brother. Seeing him was like looking into a mirror — he was who I could become if I "gave way" to my homosexuality. In my teen years, I couldn't even stomach the idea of it. Alone yet fiercely brave, my brother forged his own path and created a life for himself that I despised but subconsciously coveted. It wasn't until I came to accept myself that things between us genuinely shifted.

Bus Bullies

The worst altercations always seemed to be on the bus... because there was nowhere to run. A handful of hecklers rode my bus in the mornings and after school. Unleashing my superpower, I made friends with the bus driver, who always seemed to have my back. One time the cruelty got so bad she pulled the bus over and lectured the hecklers for what felt like an eternity. Finally, she ordered me to sit at the front of the bus to keep me safe. But the scars from that experience cut deeper than her lecture.

When I got off the bus, I told my mom what had happened and decided to call the police on the instigator, Sybil, who lived in the house in front of mine. I was desperate and didn't know where to turn. I told the police I'd been harassed so badly that they should do something about it, or I would. That threat alone brought them to my door, as well as Sybil's. It shook her up a bit, but not enough; it seemed to pour fuel on her fire as she upped her game the next day on the bus. No matter what I did, I always seemed to attract cruelty and ridicule.

Sybil was one of a handful of the kids in my town who experienced the shock of transferring to a larger school system. But, unlike my experience, she seamlessly formed alliances with other kids on campus by gaining the respect of the cool girls. What I assumed was part of her initiation, her quest to torture me fit perfectly with the survivor's playbook. We were friends in elementary school. I was part of her group of girls, and we would rotate going to each other's houses to play. We created a Spice Girls' club where each of us were members of the band (if you must know, I was Posh. I know, the writing was on the walls). She wasn't as memorable as the other girls in the group, but I found refuge in her friendship.

I always felt more comfortable being friends with girls. They seemed to be more in touch with their feelings and less rough around the edges. The girls always seemed to have more fun, while the boys just wanted to pretend to fight and talk about Ninja Turtles.

Middle school changed the dynamic between the girls and me. Most importantly, it changed my relationship with Sybil. She knew me from my younger years and was not afraid to use it as ammunition. My reputation as her friend was the perfect alibi to her relentless campaign to label me a "faggot." Sour relationships like these started the unhealthy practice of keeping people at arms-length for fear of letting anyone close enough to hurt me.

Blowing Up My Friendship

As Chris and I became closer friends, bullying and name-calling became the norm. Eventually, this led to the destruction of our friendship.

I remember my first sleepover at his house. We stayed up watching movies, playing around, and eating junk food. By 5 am, feeling tired and wanting a bit of a rest, we went to his room and laid in his bed. Aroused by our slumber party activities, we started to have a friendly wrestling match, which was the first time I felt any intimate feelings for a man. I remember the jolt of energy and excitement within me, then the instant sting of shame. I said nothing of it but thought about it constantly. Maybe those boys were right. Perhaps I was a *faggot*.

Word got out at school that we'd had a slumber party (as if we'd needed to hand the enemy any more ammo). We walked onto campus the next week as if deployed into combat in Vietnam. The steady pulse of brutality became the norm; it was expected. As lonely as it was, I couldn't imagine a world any different (a world in which I was treated with love and respect was a far-fetched fantasy to me). The teasing hurt every time, but the wounds just seemed to scab over. I could handle the fat jokes and the nerd jokes. The one that always felt like the first time, every time, was anything related to homosexuality.

I didn't want anything to do with homosexuality. I'd witnessed the harmful effects of my brother's own coming out. Not only did he suffer at the hands of his classmates, but my traditional, Middle Eastern parents were products of the psychological movement on homosexuality in the 1990s. Well-intentioned but ignorant on the subject, they decided to put my brother through therapy to talk about his homosexual feelings. As mysterious as his bullying experience was to me, so were the details of his therapy sessions. All I knew was what I saw – that it drove a wedge between my brother and my parents.

There was no way in hell I was about to go through the same thing. I was afraid of losing my parents. I'd already lost so much; what little my parents could offer in terms of affection and attention were desperately needed — they felt like my only means of survival. I needed to distance myself from any association of homosexuality, and it had to start with Chris.

The memory of the slumber party at Chris' only intensified, and fear began to consume me. The insults weren't getting any better. Instead, they got worse. Way worse. Eventually, I made an alliance with Roger, who came up with a sinister plan to perpetuate a harmful attack on Chris (to put distance between us). I was all in for it because I figured this would get me into the good graces of my accusers, and I'd be able to distance myself from any homosexual accusations. I did what I needed to do to survive, and this seemed like the only choice.

After a calculated attack on Chris that left him devastated (something I can't freely talk about to this day for how heavy it sits with me), I thought for sure I was in the clear. Little did I know that making a deal with the devil would come at a very high price. Roger almost instantly breached our alliance and continued his campaign to destroy me. It continued until high school, when I found an alternative savior.

COMING TO JESUS

My parents were well-intentioned people who lived in a culture and era that shunned homosexuality and saw it as a treatable disease. They did the best they could with what they knew. Their choice to put my brother in therapy when he opened up about his sexuality in middle school set into motion events that pointed him in a different direction than the one I imagine they'd hoped for: he ended up despising them for their betrayal. He moved in with my grandmother to finish his last couple of high school years in a neighboring city. He'd been picked on relentlessly at our school, and moving to a new one brought a world of relief to him...but it also meant I became his successor.

After witnessing how it all went down between him and my parents, I was determined to take a different path. Puberty only intensified my homosexual feelings, and this scared the living hell out of me. If I followed the same path as my brother, I thought I would die. I needed to survive, which meant I needed to hide my homosexuality at all costs.

I didn't want to become like my brother. As bad as the name-calling and bullying had been, deep down, I knew something else much worse would result from me pursuing my feelings: the loss of my parents. I knew I had homosexual feelings, but the fear of losing my father's approval prompted me to take an interest in a seemingly indirect ally: politics.

Young Republican

My dad has always been one of the most financially generous people I know. Even when he didn't have money, he provided for his family and loved ones. He would give the shirt off of his back to those in need. To this day, he is the kindest, soft-hearted human ever to walk this earth. His choice in political affiliation has thus been a mystery to me.

It was hard to know where my dad stood on anything; if poker were won simply by the look of a player's face, he would have been the world champion many times over. However, his love persisted in what he lacked in emotional provisions, he made up for in physical securities. It was a breath of fresh air whenever he expressed interest in a topic, which from what I'd seen up to that point was in either sports or politics. I had no interest in the former, so I partook in the latter.

We listened to Rush Limbaugh and watched Fox "News" together. The argumentative form of combative politics on television and radio appealed to me — hosts presented themselves as tough with strong convictions. The Republican message was straightforward: "I'm right, and you're wrong. I'm patriotic, and you're a terrorist."

Regardless of whether they were right or wrong (in fact, they were almost always wrong), it was refreshing to hear how set in their beliefs these people were. It was fascinating how skilled they were at making enemies of anyone who thought differently. Of course, this childish behavior made sense ... to a child.

I began to believe that the true enemies of our country were Hillary Clinton and Nancy Pelosi (ironically, two iconic women I now idolize). My dad and I discussed politics to no end. I memorized things Bush said on the campaign trail and celebrated with him in his victory as President of the United States. I wrote letters to Bill O'Reilly, talking about how I'd love to be on his show one day. I even read one of his books and asked him to sign it for me. I received a letter acknowledging my request and telling me to mail it to the network for signing. I have since gotten rid of that godforsaken book.

My dad and I talked about topics I knew nothing about, but the one thing I did know was that it brought us closer. For me, subscribing to all things Republican was a bonding experience with my dad, even when it was evident I had no idea what specific terms meant, like "Social Security" or "Trickle-Down Economics" (or logic, for that matter). All I knew was that I had this special bond with him, and I would do everything in my power to protect it. It was easy to believe in this simplistic form of communication that lacked any reason – the only reason I needed was to forge some sort of relationship with my dad.

But the most appealing aspect of the Republican Party, to me, was their absolute disdain and relentless war on "the gays" (clearly, I was projecting ... much like most of those in Republican leadership today). Republican politics fueled the fire of hatred of homosexuality, which created a more profound complexity within me. I was a closeted Republican who fought to no end to annihilate any association with homosexuality...while secretly looking at gay porn and covering my tracks (just like Republicans at the Ohio convention in 2016). I needed to find some sort of salvation from what felt like my most significant burden. I was wildly depressed for a kid my age — at 14, I was already contemplating suicide.

I remember one specific event in high school that prompted the pinnacle of my suicidal thoughts.

Football and Farmers

It was homecoming night at the football game. I was a freshman working the concessions stand for Future Farmers of America, an agricultural organization where I was a member. I wasn't smart enough for regular science, so I had a choice in school: I could either take "dumb" science or agriculture. The latter sounded more palatable, plus I'd be able to embark on a whole different identity as an "aggie." I was up for anything that would help me disassociate myself from homosexuality.

I'd put the horrors of middle school behind me, thinking high school would be better. Kids above me had gone through similar struggles as freshmen and faced their own demons in middle school; I hoped this had matured them and helped them move past making fun of other people.

My peers were entering new territory, as well – no longer was I the odd man out; I had survived the same three-year stretch of middle school, and we were all now in an older, bigger pool. But, as it turned out, this was wishful thinking. The older kids were just as cruel to me in high school as my peers in middle school.

I remember feeling fabulous at the homecoming game, holding a box of popcorn as I bounded up and down the bleachers with my friend Ann. Ann was a geek like me, except she seemed to avoid the cruelty of our peers. We met sometime in middle school, and we ultimately tried dating. I fondly recall us in the back of my Jeep making out. It was an exhilarating feeling to kiss a girl, but deep down, I knew it didn't feel right. Our friendship continued to grow as we realized dating wasn't for us. Although I don't recall specifics of the origin of our friendship, I remember her as being intelligent, sexy, and always captivating the attention of our teachers for her wit and charm. She was my closest female friend as we continued to nurture our friendship through the FFA.

I kept imagining what it would be like to be a cool kid — I could see them sitting in a group at the end of the bleachers, cheering for their jock friends. I kept thinking about how I could impress them. Maybe they'd think it was cool that I was here selling popcorn? I recall a strange fantasy I constantly had of the quarterback, wondering if life would ever present me the opportunity to become his savior in a moment of need. I didn't know what it took to get their attention. If I did, I would've been with them, cheering on the team instead of selling concessions.

As I approached the end of the bleachers, I couldn't believe it: the cool kids had seen me and called me over. You couldn't imagine the thoughts that raced through my head! This was my big chance. Maybe I'd say something that would make them like me. The fact that they even knew I existed was enough for me. I couldn't have been more nervous; I begged Ann to come with me, and she did.

As I got closer, I could tell exactly why they wanted to see me. They knew me, but not for any of the reasons I had hoped. They were my brother's age, and they remembered him well. It was time to pay their insults forward since he was no longer a student at the school. They had pent-up retribution to inflict, and for what seemed like an eternity, I gripped the box of popcorn as they catapulted insults at me. "Faggot," "queer," "gay," "fat," "ugly" — you name it, they spewed it.

I spiraled into paralysis as Ann grabbed my arm, dragging me away from the harassment. I was in complete shock; I hadn't seen it coming. I thought I'd turned over a new leaf in high school — that maybe for once I'd be noticed for something good. How I longed to gain their approval; I fantasized about what it would be like to run with them.

This destroyed any hope of that, all in a matter of seconds.

Ann tried to console me, but I wouldn't have it. I already thought little of myself, feeling I was at a disadvantage simply for being me. The bullies just amplified how I felt on the inside, almost like they knew who I was better than I did. I was done, so I called my dad to have him pick me up.

The instant I got into the car, I broke down. There in the passenger's seat, my hands plastered over my face, I let the floodgates loose – telling my dad how horrible those kids were to me. My dad froze. He didn't know what to say even though I could sense his concern and anxiety. When I told him what they'd said, how they'd called me a faggot, he said in what seemed at the time to be an annoyed tone, "Everyone has gay thoughts at some point, Georgie. You'll get over it!"

Another moment of shock. I didn't know what to make of this other than to close back up, retreating into myself and silently waiting for the drive to be over. It was his way of trying to console me, but it only made things worse. He did the best he could with the tools he had.

We were on the way to my grandma's house, where I spent weekends and holidays. I'd done this for as long as I could remember, and it was a tradition that continued until I moved away to college.

My grandma was already asleep by the time he dropped me off, so I went straight to the bathroom. I cleaned myself up and looked in the mirror: I was...disgusted. I kept replaying the events of the night: watching the cool kids cruelly laugh at me, standing there like a rigid board, watching their mouths move while my heart stopped. Then about what my dad said. Could this just be a blip on the radar? Was I just experiencing something I'd eventually grow out of, like acne or baby fat?

I wasn't convinced. I wondered how I could be gay, and it would ruin my life. I wanted badly to slit my wrists that night but didn't because of my fear of blood.

Not long after this incident, my depression started to get the best of me. It was evident in my personality — I lashed out more harshly at my brother and became sinisterly mischievous with friends. Life was blah and bleak, and I was going through the motions and wanted off the ride. Damn my fear of blood!

Ice Cream with Jesus

My parents instilled a strong work ethic in my siblings and me. From a young age, we worked at a restaurant located in a commercial building my grandma owned. My dad managed the property and was friends with the restaurant owner, so he got us jobs there once we each turned ten years old. We were paid in cash, and the whole thing was an excellent learning opportunity that taught me a lot about money, work ethic, and responsibility.

After reaching the ripe old age of fourteen, I decided to look for a "real" job. I was offered a position at the local ice cream parlor and began working there on weekends. It didn't take long for me to start eating my anxiety away with free ice cream. The job was also a way to escape socially; I rarely saw people from school since the shop was in the next city over. It was also in the same town as my grandma's house, a convenient refuge to get to when I spent nights at her place.

Despite being able to recreate my reputation with my co-workers, I was still acting out and spiraling – I'd taken to partying with a group of co-workers who were in college. They took me to parties in the neighboring college town, where I experienced my first beer-bong. I secretly wished I'd run into the cool kids from school at these parties, just so they'd notice me and think I was cool, too.

Meanwhile, I started to gain a different reputation with one of my co-workers, Amanda (who I later learned was a devout Christian). I mostly knew her as a nerd like me, but like my former best friend Chris, Amanda was confident in her identity. We were friendly with each other, but every time the "fun" co-workers worked with us, I changed my attitude and picked on her. It never seemed to bother her until one night, and things got a little out of hand.

Amanda was surprisingly open and honest with me about her personal life. She told me about a guy she was into who'd just returned from a mission trip (I had no idea what that was at the time). They were planning on getting dinner that night, then stopping in for ice cream. Amanda asked me to be on my best behavior since he didn't know she had feelings for him. I told her I would, and she made me promise.

Of course, I lied. The instant they walked in, I began making fun of them, saying stupid things like, "Oh, is this your *boyfriend*?" It felt good being on the other side of bullying. I felt a rush of power but regretted the whole thing as soon as they were gone. I felt extreme guilt, sensing that I'd driven them away in shame. This was before texting took off, and I didn't have Amanda's phone number, so I had no way of expressing my remorse for being such a jerk. I had to wait for an opportunity in person.

Amanda and I were scheduled to work the following day to open shop. I rarely worked mornings, and it was usually a task for just one person. I thought it was destiny — my opportunity to apologize for how horrible I'd been to her and her love interest.

I hung my head low in shame as I approached her in the back office, expressing my deepest regrets for how I'd acted. I thought she wasn't going to respond well — after all, she had every right to be upset. But, to my surprise, she cheerfully accepted my apology. Her mercy caught me by surprise. How could someone be so forgiving after such humiliation? I wouldn't have been so lovely, I thought to myself.

I thought her response would make me feel better, but it didn't. Instead, I felt even guiltier, knowing I didn't deserve such kindness. The fact is, I was a sadist when it came to shame; I could've written a manual on the subject. Feeling like I was swirling inside, the following words that came out of my mouth were: "Something is missing in my life."

I felt another jolt of shame as I shocked myself by admitting this — especially to someone like her. Our relationship wasn't that of such vulnerability, yet here I was, inflicting more shame upon myself. But she just smiled gracefully and said, "You need Jesus." I laughed at her, but deep down, I was curious.

Amanda knew the precarious position I was in — I hung out with the "rough crowd" at work, people who routinely took me to college parties and got me drunk. It was as if she saw the writing on the wall. Was I so transparent? Did she realize that *all* of my foolishness was an act of desperation? Yet, it was clear that she saw the symptoms, knew the cause, and instinctively provided the cure.

I laughed nervously; I didn't know what to say. I just walked away and did my tasks, thinking about her words: "You need Jesus."

The only thing I knew about Jesus at the time was how my grandma worshipped him. She kept a poster of him in her closet that was riddled and worn with lipstick (she kissed it every time she passed by). Her house was also littered with crucifixes, and she kept a bottle of holy water by her bedside. So, needless to say, she was digging this Jesus guy hard!

My grandma took me to church when I was a child. We'd faithfully attended the local Episcopalian church until I was old enough to say I'd "had enough" of the gay pastor and liberal teachings. It conflicted with my politics, and I wasn't going to have any more of the Sunday school bullshit nor be taught by someone who condoned homosexuality in the church. The final nail in the coffin for me was after a lesbian pastor replaced the gay pastor. My exposure to Christianity was nothing short of a political assault.

However, I always had some sort of connection to spirituality. The Sunday school teachings always sounded like folklore, yet they felt regurgitated to fit the modern era. Stories of how dinosaurs became extinct through the "great flood" because there was no room on the ark or that Moses separated the Red Sea to lead the Jewish people to safety from the Egyptians. These stories never resonated with me for how outlandish the claims were in the context of my spiritual journey. I had some early life experiences that contradicted the smallness of this god.

I vividly remember moments while lying in my bed, feeling what felt like my spirit levitating above my body. The feeling was exhilarating; it gave me a moment of reprieve from the body of pain I lived in. I gained the perspective that there was more beyond this life of torcher, that there was meaning beyond this mortal existence. These moments scared me at times, wondering why I was able to access such a connection. But the pain I was experiencing from the relentless torcher of my peers made these moments much more enticing than the feebleness of the human existence taught by the Bible. What the Bible had to offer was child's play in comparison to my own experience.

The New Cool Kids

After telling me I needed Jesus, Amanda was persistent in her requests to join her at her youth group. I finally caved, and she asked me to meet her after work one day to go together. I climbed into her beat-up car, trying to withhold both my judgment and my jokes. I peppered her with questions about what her youth group was like. Finally, she told me I just had to experience it for myself. I sat in nervous anticipation.

When we got there, I couldn't believe my eyes. The church was like no other I'd been to. It was in an industrial part of town, the church building itself housed within a large warehouse. It wasn't just the location that surprised me; it was the sheer number of cars. As men directed us on where to park, my nerves started to get the best of me. I couldn't help but think this was a much bigger deal than I'd signed up for. It felt like we were going to a special event, like a concert.

As we made our pilgrimage up to the side door of the youth group's main entrance, there were plenty of cool kids hanging outside, kicking balls and running around. It looked like recess — I never thought a church could be so cool! The crazy thing was that all these kids were there to hear about Jesus. Maybe my grandma was onto something with this Jesus character.

After a few minutes, it was time for everyone to go in and get ready for service. They turned off the lights, and the band started to play. The kids outside trickled in, and the innumerable chairs got scarce. This portion of the event was called worship, which occurred at the beginning and end of the youth group service. Worship was a time where everyone sang praise to God and prayed out loud or in groups.

The worship leader was an incredible surfer guy, and the youth pastor was on the drums. I was blown away — even the music was cool! I started getting nervous again, thinking this was too amazing to be a church and too marvelous for me. I didn't believe I deserved greatness. What was I doing here? What if I were exposed as the loser everyone at school already knew I was? I looked around at people with hands raised in the air, reaching for the sky. I saw them clapping, getting down on their hands and knees at the front of the stage. It was a lot to take in.

As I looked around, I took solace in the fact that I didn't recognize anyone. The kids were all from different schools and had no idea about me. I mean, it didn't take long for them to look at me to put me in the category of "nerdy, weird guy," but for a brief moment, I was surrounded by a group of strangers and could recreate my reputation as I did at the ice cream shop. There was nobody from my school around to expose me as a gay loser.

When the music ended, the assistant youth pastor got up to make the announcements – another cool guy. He talked about upcoming retreats and events, all of which sounded fun. After the announcements, the youth pastor came up to give the service. It was a message in the Bible about Jesus. Again, my exposure to the Bible was only what I learned from my grandma. She had an old dusty Bible that sat on the shelf, so it was strange to me that this pastor opened his and read from it. I had no idea what was in the

Bible, let alone that it was something you could learn from. Everyone around me had their own Bibles, which made me feel like a loser. I needed to get my hands on one if I were to come back to the youth group.

After the last set of worship songs, everyone was free to go. I was intrigued by this youth group and wanted to come back. Amanda told me we'd hang out a bit longer, and she'd introduce me to some people. I was scared by the offer but obliged. I stood awkwardly around these cool kids, thinking I stuck out like a sore thumb. Finally, I met the youth pastor – a muscular, bald, Mexican surfer guy who was intimidating yet friendly. I was taken aback when he knew my name. Apparently, Amanda had told him about me, and he was thankful to meet me finally.

I was shocked again — someone had talked about me behind my back but in a *positive* way? And wanted to get to know me? That was a first! Usually, it was the other way around — someone would hear about me and want nothing to do with me other than to make fun. But, I wanted this pastor to like me (as I wanted everyone there to like me), so I promised I'd be back.

Coming to Jesus

It took a few visits for me to finally "come to Jesus." On my third visit during the service, I was presented with the "salvation message." A salvation message is meant for newcomers and unbelievers. Usually preached at special events like Easter or Christmas, it's the message about how you get into heaven. Church members (called "believers") are encouraged to invite their "unbelieving" friends and family members to hear the message of salvation.

The salvation message is the message that says that we, as a human race, were introduced to sin in the Garden of Eden when Eve took the fruit of temptation from the Serpent (the devil in disguise). After this original sin, God cast them out of the Garden of Eden, and the rest of humanity became outcasts from God. According to the message, the only way to God is through Jesus, who is the perfect person — God in the flesh — who sacrificed himself for the entire world. Anyone willing to confess their sins and take Jesus as their lord can join him in heaven when they die for all eternity. Those who reject Jesus go to hell for all of eternity.

This message was appealing, but most importantly, it meant I could come back to this group of people, and they would accept me. I felt like I belonged there, so I decided to oblige and commit my life to Jesus.

I was enjoying getting to know these new cool kids. They were lovely — by which I mean they weren't talking shit about me to my face or calling me faggot. Instead, they seemed to take a genuine interest in me. But it didn't take long to figure out that they were just like the cool kids at school, except that at least the kids at school were bold enough to make their revile clear and public. By contrast, the youth group kids disguised it; they "Christianized" it (a term commonly used to describe cliché Christian terms).

There were many different cliques in the youth group, similar to the ones at school. You had the preppy kids, the surfer kids, the jocks, the nerds, and the weirdos. I was considered a weirdo and spent most of my time with the girls. I gravitated to girls because I felt most comfortable with them. All the cool guys were handsome and intimidating. I didn't want to expose myself to their disdain, so I found myself in a gaggle of girls. As it turned out, Christian girls were just as cruel as secular girls, but they were cunning about it. Eventually, I formed my tribe with these girls and resented when the pastor broke us into prayer groups along gender lines when I was forced to go with the guys.

There were many moments that I felt like an outsider. Being relegated to the weird category of the social groups, I constantly felt like a burden in the presence of greatness. The patriarchal hierarchy was alive and well in the Christian faith, and the youth group was no exception. One winter at a Christian camp, we were segregated by gender in our cabins. We were told that there was no purple allowed at all (boys being blue and girls being pink, we couldn't comingle in the cabins together). One night, the boys decided to strip the bunk beds of the mattresses to form a wrestling ring. Everyone got their shot, showing off their immaculate sport and muscle. I'd be lying if I said that it didn't turn me on to see muscular men take their shirts off and wrestle around with each other.

Eventually, it became my turn. I could hear the laughter of the boys as they chanted for me to take off my shirt. That was an absolute no in my book. I was still widely insecure about my body, having developed female breast tissue at an early age (a clinical diagnosis known as gynecomastia). It was the primary source of my shame for many years. I recall being a junior counselor for a summer day camp while I was in middle school. We went to the public pool to take the kids for a swim. As I jumped into the pool with my shirt on, the lifeguard blew his whistle. The entire attendees were staring at me as if I had antlers growing out of my skull.

I tried to explain to the lifeguard that I couldn't take my shirt off, coming up with every excuse under the sun. Finally, he told me that it was the pool rules, and if I was to partake in the activities, I had to take my shirt off. No exceptions. During this shameful incident, the adult counselors had called my dad to come to my assistance. There he stood on the other side of the fence, beaconing me to him. I held my head low, tears rolling down my face as I shamefully walked over to meet him. He implored me to take my shirt off, telling me it wasn't a big deal. I cried harder, telling him I couldn't do that. He eventually took me home as my back faced the curious eyes behind me.

My dad was well aware of this insecurity. I recall him taking me to endless doctor's visits, being told that I would eventually "grow out of it," and it was just "baby fat." I was told by many doctors that I was too young for plastic surgery and to just wait it out. But when puberty hit, the quarter-shaped pouches of fat sat behind my nipples relentlessly. As I advanced to high school, I developed tips and tricks for avoiding taking my shirt off. Wearing undershirts for PE and refusing to go to pool parties were just a couple of my tactics. This insecurity followed me into my mid-twenties when shortly after moving back home from leaving the church, I booked an appointment with a plastic surgeon and had them removed for good.

* * *

Back at camp, the guys laughed at my timidness and retreated to their orders. I entered the makeshift ring and was assigned a challenger. They thought it would be funny to see timid me wrestle with the muscular youth pastor. He was built like a semi, constantly bragging about his 250lb frame. It took a matter of seconds before I was taken down to the ground, pinned in humiliation. I was shaking more from the shock of it all than the impact. I couldn't believe what just happened. I thought to myself, *who are these guys that they would poke fun at the weak chubby kid?* After all, these were supposed Christians. It brought back memories from middle school and my former torture.

From that day on, I vowed never to put myself in such a position to receive such a humiliating reception.

THOUGHT: THE CONCEPT OF SALVATION

The whole premise of the Christian faith rests on salvation — the belief that you're too wretched for your own good and require saving from your sins. This explains why someone struggling with low self-esteem (like me) would turn to a belief system that claims to have answers to life's most challenging questions. Much of Evangelical Christianity hones in on the insecurities of humans, telling them they're sinners who need forgiveness. Their individual sins (a whole litany of possibilities) are just the result of the one actual sin: our separation from God.

One doesn't truly understand the weight that the concept of sin places on a person until it is packaged in the context of eternity and damnation. Essentially, you're told that you're repulsive in the sight of your creator and destined for eternal damnation for the acts of ancestors thousands of years removed. Their rebellion became your burden, and the human race was sentenced to eternal damnation. Your ticket to heaven, then, is obtained only through admitting that sin is what caused our collective separation from God and that the acts of a perfect God-human (Jesus) are the only things that will fulfill God's plan. Jesus' sacrifice on the cross was the down payment on the redemption of those who would believe in him from then on. His perfection transformed our imperfection, making us "white as snow" and allowing us to enter into heaven for all eternity. Those who reject this message of salvation are condemned to an eternity of damnation in hell.

Christianity teaches that God loved us so much that he sent his perfect son to die in our stead, to bear the weight of wrath that was destined for us. All you must do is accept Jesus as your Lord and devote your life to him. This is all to highlight the radicalness of a perfect God's love for his creation, who should be eternally grateful for his grace. This subconsciously instills a guilt complex in the believer, who knows their salvation is contingent on the actions of a perfect man who died for them. You know there's nothing you, the sinner, can do on your own merit other than to devote your life to God. Complete and utter dependency.

Due to this belief system, I felt like I was unworthy of anything good. Whatever good I received was strictly by the grace of God — a blessing. I believed I wasn't worthy enough to be loved simply for being myself because who I was was sinful. According to my faith, I was repulsive and would be lucky to end up with a wife and kids should God ever bless me with any.

So it stood to reason that my sin of homosexuality was an abomination before God, and if I were to act upon it, it would be a complete blaspheme to what God intended. I would suffer eternal damnation if I fulfilled my "lusts" and eventually assigned to hell for all eternity for rejecting God's order. This is not to say that all Christian denominations adopt such militant beliefs, but Evangelicals took it to the next level among those who did.

I constantly found myself alongside my fellow "brothers and sisters in Christ," kneeling or fully prostrating myself on the ground in front of the stage at church, begging for God's forgiveness. We wallowed in our wretchedness as people badly in need of God. I'd walk up to the prayer team standing on the sides of the stage to confess my sins and ask for prayers of forgiveness. Our prayers were constantly filled with things like, "God, I know I'm unworthy of your love. I don't deserve it." These prayers created a psychological dysmorphia that has been single-handedly the most challenging obstacle to overcome in my life. I still bear the scars today.

I was ripe for the picking, being young and extremely insecure. I hit my lowest point — depressed and wanting to kill myself — at age fourteen. I couldn't bear the thought of myself, so this message, which confirmed what I felt, became my everything. I didn't think I deserved any better – I was a fat, gay kid nobody liked. I was picked on for being different, so the conditional love the church presented to me was appealing. If I confessed my sins, these people would let me into their group. I could earn their love by showing my devotion to the faith. I could "work out my own salvation with fear and trembling," knowing I was doing good before God and others.

Form of Control

After extensive experience and study, I believe the following: The Christian church, as created by Paul, disciples of Jesus, and other men who supposedly wrote the New Testament, was used by various societies to control the masses. It is common knowledge in the historian community that religion was created to handle groups as civilizations began to grow. As communities grew and became more advanced, religion became a means for promoting assistance and cooperation amongst its members.

Christianity gained traction globally as Constantine paved the way to have the Roman Empire inevitably adopt Christianity as its national religion. The Roman Empire was the most powerful empire of its time. Controlling a majority of the known advanced world, the Roman Empire became a catalyst for the advancement of Christianity. I believe that, because of the many rules laid upon Christian believers, it was easy to stoke fear in citizens and thus make them obedient. Romans were known for their conquests and control. What better way to control the masses than to have a monotheistic deity be the final word when it came to the rule of law? It was brilliant, really, yet extraordinarily destructive and harmful to the evolution of the human race.

I experienced that firsthand. For years I believed my true nature resulted from "the fall" – Adam and Eve eating the forbidden fruit, an act that caused the whole human race to be excommunicated from God. My homosexuality (supposedly addressed in the book of Romans) was also a result of sin — "exchanging the natural use of a woman ... burning in lust for other men." This was (and remains) the central passage used by Christians as a weapon against the gay community and justify virulent homophobia (more on this later). Many other verses (written by patriarchal individuals) were (and still are) used to control women, children, and more.

Dismantling the System

My commitment to this belief system (for a large part of my life) had me constantly needing to try not to pick myself apart and tell myself what a horrible person I was. *"I'd be so lucky to have a good job that I enjoy or be loved by a man who I deserve."* These thoughts were more potent in the years just after I left the faith. I woke up in night sweats, thinking I was making a huge mistake — that the life I'd chosen to leave was exemplary all along and that if I didn't return to God, I'd go to hell. The fear and intimidation of the faith were so embedded in my psyche that it still haunts me to this day (though it has lost its sting, so to speak).

Where this belief system still has its power is in the way I view myself. There are plenty of moments where I start to doubt my worthiness of anything good. Whether it be on a date or in my profession, thoughts about who I am seem to dictate my behaviors in a way that is self-destructive. When I experience some level of rejection, I go internal. I question the validity of my own wants and needs, telling myself that I am not worthy of such good things because who I am is desperately wicked and deceived. Desiring something good becomes a chore, having to retrain my brain in knowing that the principles of Christianity are no longer relevant in how I view myself, and thus are worthy of great and wonderful things.

A great deal of therapy and energy work has helped give me the tools needed to dismantle this mindset. It's not that it has been completely eradicated from my life; that couldn't be further from the truth. But years of healing have helped me find my way through joys and dislikes I've discovered are my own. I apply concepts learned in therapy to build a bit more confidence, day by day, living my truth and developing my own voice.

MAKINGS OF A NEW CREATION

My newfound faith was a turning point for me as I entered my sophomore year of high school. The youth group was great, but I needed something more substantial. One of the girls in the youth group mentioned that she and some other high schoolers attended the college group on Friday nights and invited me to join them. I was introduced to some cool college-aged people, who ended up taking me under their wings once they heard I was a "new believer."

I loved this new group. They seemed much more mature than the high schoolers. They were fun and exciting, and most of them went to the famous local Bible college in town. I quickly became friends with a group that was just like me — nerdy. We went to In-N-Out after church service and stayed up late, talking about random things. I felt at

home with these friends and quickly drank the Kool-Aid —
I pimped out both my Bible and my Jeep with the church's
branding & Jesus propaganda and bought countless books
on the Christian faith. I was skyrocketing towards greatness
in the church, showing a level of interest close to psycho
boyband stalkers. I couldn't get enough of the church and
the people in it.

Yet, just as excitement bloomed, the reality of my darkest sin constantly kept me in check. I hid the books I
bought on homosexuality since it seemed an unforgivable
sin. Those preaching talked continuously about the follies
of granting marriage to homosexuals, how it would open
the floodgates of pedophilia and beastiality. I was scared
shitless of these associations. I couldn't imagine how anyone could be attracted to a child, let alone an animal! Unfortunately, this perverse mindset still permeates the
minds of many in the Evangelical community. But this was
my biggest fear if word got out that I struggled with homosexuality: that I'd be treated like a child molester. So I hid
my secret for a while, until one night after a particular service.

Coming Out Christian

One day it was announced that a girl on the leadership
team would give her testimony to the entire college group

for the first time. It was apparently a juicy story, so it was to be quite the event. I took my seat as worship started, curious to hear what this woman was hiding that she was finally going to reveal.

After the announcements, Pastor Joe started to give a lesson on Romans 1. It was the most significant text about the church and homosexuality. He preached on how homosexuality was a sin and listed out reasons why. He had my undivided attention – it hit closer to home than anyone could have imagined. Sure, my friends knew about my homosexual brother who "didn't know the Lord," but they didn't know anything about my homosexual feelings.

I was both fascinated and frightened — fascinated by how precise the Bible seemed to be in addressing the subject of homosexuality and frightened that I would get discovered. I hung on every word the pastor spoke, furiously highlighting in my Bible and taking notes on specific things he said. Meanwhile, my fears mounted in anticipation of the special guest.

About half an hour into the sermon, Joe asked a woman in the crowd to come to the microphone. So here it was, the event of the night! She started telling her story – how she was happily married (I don't remember whether she had kids) and felt the Lord was calling her to share her testimony with the entire group, to show how God worked and continued to work in her life. She was raised in a perplex-

ing family situation, resulting in one of her biggest struggles: homosexuality. If she didn't have my attention before,
she had it now.

She continued to talk about how she struggled with homosexuality for quite some time, apparently due mainly
to her upbringing. Finally, she shared how she was healed
from homosexuality and was now pursuing a life committed to God. She told us that the Lord had provided her with
a husband and family that loved and embraced her. I kept
thinking about how I longed to have her story but knew I
had to do my part by confessing my sin to start the process
of healing. I wasn't ready to do it that night, but I listened
raptly, hoping that one day I could be as brave as her.

After service, she made her way to the back of the
church, where she was immediately surrounded by people
giving her praise and adoration. I wanted badly to speak
with her as I orbited around, and I was intrigued by how she
had overcome her darkest sin — to the point of being open
about it. But my insecurities got the best of me that night,
and I just thanked her for her bravery.

Thought: Homosexuality as a Mental Illness

The association of pedophilia and beastiality with homosexuality recategorizes it as a mental illness. Quite lit-

erally, in 1973, the American Psychiatric Association voted to remove "ego-syntonic homosexuality" as a mental disorder. Before its removal, homosexuals were treated just like any other patient with mental illnesses. This pervasive diagnosis has lingered in our community, causing psychological deformities in those who struggle with homosexual feelings.

The efforts of the LGBTQ Civil Rights Movement have done wonders in shifting the homosexual association with these stigmas, yet this old belief lingers among many in the Evangelical faith. Such associations demonize and dehumanize homosexuals, causing a "righteous anger" towards the "sin of homosexuality." In their perverse minds, the cause of dismantling the "gay agenda" is a righteous one, saving the most vulnerable souls in our communities. Consequently, associations of the like maintain the biases and discrimination against LGBTQ individuals, thus invalidating the human rights of those who need protection the most.

This leads to a much more significant, more sinister plot by the Evangelicals. Considered "pro-life," one would think their Christian duty to care for the down-and-out would be to advocate for mental health and other human rights resources rather than strip away civil rights from vulnerable groups. The hypocrisy is baffling. Believing that they have a "higher calling" to be "examples of Jesus," so often they curse his name. Acting more like the religious zealots Jesus condemned (the Pharisees), they are quick to judge and unrelenting on protecting their rights over human rights. When confronted, they interpret this as "persecution for their faith," unable to step out of their perspective to see it through the eyes of real human beings. You know, like Jesus so often did.

My Own "Coming Out"

After some time, I built up the courage to speak with someone about my homosexuality. I was still ashamed to admit that I had homosexual feelings, but I knew the first step to healing was to confess this sin. I contemplated who I would entrust with this news and had a few people in mind. I knew I had to open up to a woman first because that would make me more comfortable.

After joining the college group, I thought about a couple who served in the youth group I got to know better. I loved the girlfriend — she was fun, lighthearted, and outspoken. She exuded a confidence I coveted. When I pulled her aside one night to tell her my secret, she told me I should probably talk to her boyfriend; she said it was a sin more suitable to confess to a man. I was nervous about the idea but told her I would.

I thought about how to approach him, hoping she'd at least given him a heads up. I was still uncomfortable around men, thinking they'd wig out around me. This was a common fear based on reality. The hyper aggression towards homosexuals in the Evangelical space of the time was more radical than today (hard to believe, right?). Then, one night at the college group, I felt a sense of guilt that I attributed to the Holy Spirit "convicting me" for not coming clean, so I prayed to be given the courage to talk to him. It worked: I pulled the boyfriend aside before service and asked if we could go to a quieter space. He said he'd be happy to, so we headed into the kid's ministry area...and I told him.

He looked like a deer in headlights; apparently, his girlfriend hadn't given him the heads-up. I could see the awkwardness on his face, then in his voice. I don't remember his exact words, but I could tell he was uncomfortable with my confession. I felt deep shame for sharing and heavily restated how I was pursuing healing, which was why I was telling him. I felt like I was admitting to some sort of sinister crime, or worse, being a child molester (for context, I was only about fifteen years old).

I immediately felt I'd been too honest and vulnerable with this man, and my insecurities got the best of me. How I experienced so much shame for confessing a "sin" still boggles my mind. I feared most his interpretation that my homosexuality meant I was attracted to him, or worse, children! Determined to distance myself from this couple, I sought to become closer to others in the group who didn't know my secret yet. I gravitated towards women even more out of fear that my male friends would think I was attracted to them. This became a common trait of mine — backing away from people with whom I felt I'd been too vulnerable, especially men. (This is something I still work on today in friendships with men).

Ultimately, I decided that night would be the last time I'd share my darkest sin with anyone. It wouldn't be until college that I would ever tell anyone about it again.

God Votes Republican

Not long after I joined the college group, Pastor Joe announced that he was ending his pastoral duties with the college ministry to start a new church in the hometown of my high school called Real Life Church. This was his hometown, too, and he had graduated from the same high school. This news couldn't have come at a better time. I'd become enamored with his teaching style and "oh-so-cool" ways, and I thought this could be my opportunity to shine.

I wanted badly to win over the affections of this pastor and those in his inner circle. If I could pull it off, it would be a massive leap in status among my peers (or so I thought).

Where I once was the awkward, gay, fat kid in middle school and freshman in high school, I was fast becoming the bois- terous, intelligent, Republican Christian (I'd lost the weight, too; I was like the Christian Jenny Craig. There's nothing a diet of self-hate and judgment can't fix).

It also was an asset that Real Life Church was politically aligned with my ideals. The church was riding the tides of the movement of Evangelical participation in political "jus- tice," and I frequently attended seminars on Bible prophecy and "signs of the times" conferences (sometimes, I even brought my dad along). These seminars were filled with rhetoric on current events that endorsed the Republican narrative. God was for Israel, and so was the Republican Party, while Democrats believed in breaking up God's promised land between the Palestinians (descendants of Ishmael — son of the adultery by Abraham) and Israelis (descendants of Isaac — God's chosen people and heirs to the promised land of Israel). Thus, Democrats were the en- emy of Israel, and consequently, God.

The institution's skirting of the line between church and state went so far as to inform congregants of the bib- lical stance on specific political issues, presenting a flyer with both political viewpoints but referencing verses that clearly supported the Republican view. Abortion and guns were a no-brainer — they believed in the right to life until you were a kid gunned down by an active shooter, in which case a good guy with a gun would fix the problem. Most of these verses were a clear stretch of the imagination, and had they been put up to any type of theological test, they would have failed miserably. But to the submissive flock, this was palatable.

For example, the war in Iraq was justified by a poem in the Old Testament. The ramifications for outspokenly believing anything other than the Republican party line were dire, to the point that your faith could be questioned. Not only was it unpatriotic to not support the war efforts of President Bush, but it was also ungodly.

This American Republican Christian pseudo-identity served me well. I was able to make outlandishly unjustifiable claims devoid of reality with a solid and unearned sense of confidence (after all, the Bible was the source of absolute truth). I bought all the books I could on hermeneutics (Bible interpretation, literally, "justification for the faith.") I found websites addressing some of Christianity's most important questions and printed articles that supported my claims of faith. I collected anything I could get my hands on.

Wherever "facts" were limited, faith could step in. I mastered the art of taking an argument to the brink of apparent defeat and reviving it with "faith." I could be knee-deep in discussion with all the facts and reality stacked against me, and somehow all it took was to invoke faith; we were merely feeble humans, while God was the creator — who were we to challenge the way God did things?

For example, for the unanswerable question, "if God is good, why does He allow evil?" I had my lines down: multiple sources talk about how we, as human beings, chose to walk away from God, thus allowing sin to enter the world. This gave an opening to defend the Bible (the Bible referred to as the actual "Word of God"). I recited "facts" I found through multiple sources on Christian archeology, geography, history – any form of pseudo-science to manifest my most excellent argument in defense of the faith. I turned confirmation bias into a sport!

If that wasn't good enough and I found myself backed into a corner, I would say, "Well, God is God, so who am I to challenge his Word?" This was the best way to end an argument: the indestructible claim that the Bible was the authoritative Word of God, so whatever was contained in it was absolute (even if it was sometimes incomprehensible to mortals). Of course, this left the opposition scratching their heads. Most of the time, I knew the Bible better than the person I was arguing with, so they couldn't refute or invalidate what I said. In my Christian faith, I thought this was God using me to "confound the wise, using the foolish things of the world," but as I stepped away from the Christian faith, I realized it was more of a way to retreat from arguing with a drunk.

At the same time, I needed some sort of tangible proof for what I believed because if anyone had pulled back the curtain, they would've seen my fear that everything I believed in was wrong. My enthusiastic support of the church's stance on homosexuality at the time was in part because if the faith was false and homosexuality wasn't a sin (or curable), I'd be forced to accept the fact that I was gay.

And if I *were* gay, I thought there'd be no place for me in my family. So actively arguing the "facts" of faith was my way of maintaining the façade, a revelation that came to me while watching a documentary on a cult years later, after leaving the faith (God sure works in mysterious ways).

At the time, fear only made me press in deeper.

Chemistry and Christ

I constantly talked about my faith in class. I often held heated debates with my English and Chemistry teachers, defending the faith. Of course, they constantly questioned the premise of my faith. Still, my tenacity in training for rebuttals to popular secular belief systems frequently had me appear victorious (frankly, the teachers knew they were dealing with a student operating on a different plane of reality, so it was easier for them to let me win battles, knowing they'd already won the war).

My most prized conquest was my Chemistry teacher, who'd taught at the school since my pastor had been a student. Pastor Joe recalled moments with this teacher, remembering him as a curmudgeon and a fierce opponent to the faith. Things hadn't changed much over fifteen years, and it was my time to become David to this Goliath.

He constantly belittled Christians and anyone who believed in creationism. So I did my homework on the subject before entering his class, prepared to take on this heathen by quoting famous Christian "scientists" like Ken Ham and Louie Giglio (spoiler alert: they don't have science degrees).

Ken Ham is a creationism proponent who became famous for building a multi-million-dollar ark in the middle of nowhere. He spent millions on a museum to commemorate mythical stories and "facts" — money that would've been better spent sheltering homeless human beings. He also gained attention when humiliated in a nationally broadcast debate with Bill Nye. Have fun Googling this monster!

My debates with my chemistry teacher got so heated that he sometimes changed the lesson of the day just to get into it with me or asked me to stay after class so we could continue arguing. I could tell I got under his skin at times and interpreted this as "the Holy Spirit working to convict him" (Evangelicals believe that one of the roles of the Spirit of God, a member of the "holy trinity," is constantly moving on the hearts of nonbelievers to give them signs to bring them to accept the faith).

One time it got so intense that he solicited the assistance of the neighboring biology teacher to defend his stance since I was unrelenting in mine. But, of course, it didn't matter; what he said went in one ear and out the other. He must have thought I was an attentive student, though, because he always seemed to pay me respect by thoughtfully listening to what I had to say, even though he never, ever agreed with me.

Getting Him Saved

My ultimate goal in our debates was to get this teacher to come to know Jesus. During my first Easter service at the church, Pastor Joe announced that events for the holiday would be held at my high school. This was meaningfully symbolic – the church had established itself in town, and the high school was the community center. This would be great publicity for the church, and since Pastor Joe had attended the school himself, it was nostalgic for him. It was expected to be a well-publicized event, and the congregation was ecstatic at the news — no one more so than me.

There are two major holidays that Evangelicals seize upon to preach the "salvation message" (the one to get non-believers to accept Jesus as their savior): Christmas and Easter. These are symbolic holidays — Christmas for Jesus' birth and Easter for his death on the cross, and subsequent rise from the grave three days later.

I was determined to get my chemistry teacher to show up so he'd hear the salvation message and be convicted by the Spirit to commit his life to God. I also thought this would earn me brownie points with the church leadership. When I talked to Pastor Joe about inviting him, he was intrigued but skeptical. He remembered how hard-headed this teacher was. I thought this was just icing on the cake: this was my opportunity to show my pastor I was worthy of the task!

I hounded my teacher about the service, begging him to come. He gave me grief, but when I handed him a flyer and asked him to consider it, I saw a glimmer of hope. Plus, as we continued with our banter in class, I caught the attention of the junior varsity star quarterback, who also attended my church but had never really noticed me until my argumentative moments in class. It felt amazing to team up with him to try and get our teacher to come to the Easter service.

As it turned out, our teacher did end up coming! We couldn't have been more overjoyed. Of course, nothing changed after that, but the accolades I received for getting him to attend the service were enough to satisfy my soul. I was also getting recognized by classmates for the first time (in a good light).

Debate Team

I was so convincing in my arguments that the debate team decided to make me the star competitor in their lunchtime election debate. Despite not being a club member, they asked me to be the opposition party candidate, John Kerry (during the 2004 election season). Everyone at school knew how devoted I was to my faith and the Republican Party.

I constantly debated with liberal teachers about the war efforts in Iraq, parroting information I got from watching Brit Hume, Bill O'Reilly, and Hannity & Colmes on Fox "News" every evening with my dad. When confronted with skepticism about how I could be a Christian and support such a despicable war, I quoted Bible verses (taken wildly out of context) or changed the subject. I didn't care, nor did my classmates; they didn't know the difference, and I didn't care to explain. I could have been a great politician, which is probably why the debate team wanted me to play the part.

At the first invite to debate, I said no because I took it as an insult to my love of George W. Bush. Moreover, I couldn't imagine playing John Kerry. After all, I knew nothing about him, and I wasn't willing to do the research (this was a common theme when confronted with facts and reason – I'd just ignore them or turn away). But, eventually, I accepted the role under one condition: I could mock John Kerry while playing him. Ultimately, the team received my terms, and I was set for the debate.

The debate turned out to be a circus. The classroom was packed to watch me debate the person playing George W. Bush: an intelligent liberal who had done his homework. I found myself pulling up notes I'd made the night before, mostly making character jabs rather than substantive political arguments. This was my tactic: avoid discussing policy by attacking Kerry's reputation. It's no different from what we see in politics today: using tactics like gaslighting or character slander to avoid describing support for a controversial platform. I was successful in my attempts. After about ten minutes, I was excused for lack of substance. Another win as I felt that I had succeeded in my endeavors.

Future Farmers of America

As I started developing a name for myself at school, I won over the affections of the most prominent social group on campus: my Mexican classmates. Although I was considered white, I wasn't like the rest of the preppy, popular white people. Instead, I identified more as a minority because the minorities were more friendly, open, and fun to be around. I also was more accessible than the stale white crowd.

I began to have a charismatic personality, something I learned to develop with my newfound identity as a Christian. Believing I had the answers to life's most challenging questions brought zeal and resilient confidence. When times were hard, I found strength in my faith, which helped me get through it. This allowed me to form a personality of dynamic character and unsubstantiated confidence.

Although well-known, I was still considered a loner — I had no group of friends. I found myself in the same predicament as middle school: I had nowhere to go at lunch besides teachers' classrooms. What was different in high school was that I didn't feel like I had to fight for my life from the harassment of bullies. Wanderer that I was, in my early high school years, I felt at home with the Future Farmers of America (FFA) and assumed the identity of being an "aggie."

The FFA was a reprieve from daily life. Through it, I could jet off to competitions around the state, which allowed me to escape the bubble of my community. In addition, I met people at different schools who didn't know my status on my campus and vice versa, so we accepted one another as we were. Of course, my identity as a Republican Christian was not absent in this environment — I expressed my faith and beliefs quite often. And as it was a traditionally conservative organization, I was received quite well.

I was enamored by the structure of the FFA and desired to pursue leadership roles early on. I made a name for myself at my local chapter, which got me recognition on the regional level. When I ran for regional office at the end of my sophomore year, I won. It felt fantastic to be liked enough to win an election finally. I became acquainted with the other regional leaders, and we hit it off. I felt like these people were my family.

We met for our first regional meeting at the president's home in central California. We conducted our business in the daytime, then got up to shenanigans in the evenings. Despite our different upbringings or areas we came from, we forged a bond more profound than anything I had previously imagined. This was mainly due to the regional director, a jolly Santa Claus type figure. He constantly made us laugh, but we learned quickly to never get on his bad side.

He pushed us hard, and we obliged. He became one of the kindest and most caring people in my life.

Burning Bridges

As a staunch Christian, it was common for my beliefs to get in the way of connection in my relationships. Eventually, my friendship with the regional director ended because of, you guessed it, his homosexuality. Years after I graduated, I kept in contact with this man. When we got together, we reminisced about the past, and he asked me to participate in certain regional events. At the time, I was big into photography, so he asked me to attend significant regional events to take photos of the participants and activities.

As I got deeper into my faith, I formed a stricter stance on homosexuals. Unfortunately, our relationship was severed after asking me to ordain a civil union between him and his partner. Honored by this request, yet knee-deep in Bible college at the time and having assumed pastoral roles at Bayside Church (more to come on that), I inquired with Pastor Ryan, the senior pastor at Bayside, on how to handle this request.

Ryan clarified what I was to do: the Bible was unambiguous about homosexuality. I knew that if I disobeyed Ryan's orders, I'd be ridiculed and ostracized if anyone ever found out. With a heavy heart, I replied to this man with whom I had a strong bond that no, it was, in fact, a contradiction and an offense to my faith to marry him and his partner, regardless of how flattered I was that he'd asked.

This was the last time I ever heard from him. This is one of the most regrettable losses of friendships I have ever experienced – even more than Chris, my childhood best friend.

My New Nature

No matter where I went or what I did, my faith was my rock and foundation. As I continued to learn, I found myself identifying even more with the principles of the faith, and it became the essence of my entire being.

It was the tool that got me through my greatest struggles. Top of the list, of course, was my issue with homosexuality. I still had this sin to deal with, but the more I leaned into my faith, the less distracting my homosexual feelings became. I read books on homosexuality that said it was the most repulsive of sins since it defied the very existence and purpose of God's creation. Stupid shit like, *God created Adam and Eve, not Adam and Steve.* I found literature that helped me understand it better through the eyes of the Christian faith and began to despise homosexuality to its core.

Love the sinner, hate the sin is a common phrase used by church people. It's a way of expressing resentment for the "evil" in people's lives while maintaining that the grievance comes from a place of love for that person, not judgment. It's a classic way of absolving any responsibility for a critical judgment of someone to "hate your sin because I love you."

This refined my self-hating complex — learning that I had two natures. My old nature was out to destroy me and represented my sin; my new nature was rooted in Jesus and represented his forgiveness and freedom to enter heaven. We were constantly told in sermons that we had a choice to feed one nature or the other, but not both. Whichever nature we chose to feed would result in us sinning more or less, and it was my duty to feed my new nature with the "Word of God," and stay in fellowship with other believers. We were encouraged to be "in the world but not of the world," meaning that we were to be a light to the darkness of the world, not partake in evil.

This belief that I had two natures was a turning point in my view of my homosexuality. I saw the old nature as no longer me — it was a relic of the past. When I was tempted to sin, I chalked it up to the old nature being hungry. I had a choice: I could feed it by looking at gay porn or fantasizing about men, or read the Bible and feed my new nature. It was a reinforcement to abandon my true self, to run away from who I feared I would become. The more I focused on the new nature, the more I realized how powerful I had become because of Jesus or how weak I would be without him.

The "new nature" belief gave me power in many respects. Even the stings of the bullies seemed to subside; Roger became more like a yapping dog than a ferocious beast. Sure, he and others picked on me from time to time, but confidence started welling up within me, prompting me to fight back.

One time one of the most ruthless bus bullies, sitting behind me at the time, said, "George, you're so gay." I turned around and retorted, "So if I was, are you interested? Are *you* the one who's gay?" He shut up immediately, and by the time he tried again, I had my own nickname for him that made him the gay one. Realizing my new nature gave me the confidence to rise above; my faith became a great tool to find meaning outside my true identity. I had finally found a coping mechanism to survive my world of torcher. After that, there was no turning back.

A Refuge

As I entered junior year, I realized there was no Christian group on campus, and to my knowledge, there never had been. A handful of classmates were professed Christians, but their religious identities were soon relinquished when they walked onto campus.

Everyone had their clique, assimilating to the "ways of the world" (things not of God but the secular community; predominantly sinful). I felt it my duty to break the bonds between us — to unite us in our faith rather than our social status. Forming a Christian group was my attempt to be a part of something — to finally belong. This is part of why I named the group Refuge.

We held our first meeting in the classroom of a teacher who professed to be Christian. I did my homework: I'd gotten the new club announced in the school bulletin, posted flyers about it around school, and set up a booth to hand out proselytizing materials. Enthusiasm was scarce, especially since having a Christian group on campus exposed some of the cool kids who said they were believers but didn't want friends to be weirded out by their faith. I didn't care — I was set to bring us together by drawing a line in the sand.

Our numbers grew as I persevered in my marketing and recruiting efforts. I asked Pastor Joe to come to speak to the group. He was excited about the opportunity and praised me for my accomplishments in setting up a group on campus but asked the assistant pastor to attend instead due to a scheduling conflict. I decided to get pizza for the event to attract an even bigger crowd. People who hadn't been initially to our meetings were in attendance, and the room was packed. I wasn't sure whether it was the pastor or the pizza, but whatever it was, it worked!

Eventually, I asked one of the popular freshman girls to join and become my protégé. She and I were both in the school choir, and I was fascinated by her popularity. She'd arrived on campus just as I approached my senior year, so it made sense to pass the torch on to her, entrusting her to steer the group in my absence. She took on the role of co-leader, and we were finally a full-fledged club. I felt like we'd accomplished something great, and even better, I thought I'd scored brownie points with the leadership at Real Life Church by starting the first Christian group on campus.

Itching to Get Out

By the time I reached my last year of high school, I had a bad case of senioritis. At this point, I'd formed bonds with people throughout the state in the FFA — people who actually wanted to know me for me. I was climbing the leadership ladder and found myself eager to try my hand at state leadership. This would require me to take a year off from college, but my devotion to the organization made the decision a no-brainer. I thought of my senior year titles as steppingstones to bigger and brighter things. My future aspirations also caused me to neglect my duties as senior class president.

Even though I won senior class president and was voted "Most Spirited" in the senior class yearbook, my heart wasn't in it. It was more of a power move to beat the (formerly) unopposed popular white boy and flex my influence amongst my peers. As soon as I won, I moved on to the next thing, ditching the lunchtime Associated Student Body meetings. The rest of the senior class officers were popular kids who yielded their influence and friendship to my power, so I thought rather than fight them on it, I'd let them have the win.

I didn't care. A result of my apathy for my peers and title was that my senior class never got their ten-year reunion. My peers had put me through hell in my younger years, and I thought this was appropriate retribution. I didn't care to see them ever again after graduation and knew they felt the same. The lack of respect was mutual.

My Last Hurrah

I felt powerful in my new life. I had shaped an image that appeared to conquer any trial I faced. The narrative was once that I was a weak homosexual kid who was bullied daily. Now, I was a strong, confident leader. Although my peers never really accepted me, I did feel a sense of control. If they left me alone, then I left them alone.

The administration was keenly aware of my tenacity around my faith — especially our hardass vice principal. We had a love/hate relationship. He was a staunch Republican, so we connected on that level, but Evangelical Christianity came between us. Nevertheless, I constantly found myself conversing with him, trying to get him to see my side of things. We had an unusual relationship of respect: he respected my tenacity, and I admired him, too. So I thought I'd exercise my clout with him by requesting to speak at senior graduation.

Traditionally, only the ASB president and valedictorian were slated for speeches at graduation. I was neither, but I still felt I deserved a spot for my accomplishments in winning senior class president and my leadership endeavors in the Future Farmers of America. So, after a contentious discussion with him and the rest of ASB leadership, I was approved to speak. There was just one condition: my speech was to be agreed beforehand for fear of going off the rails into *Christianland.*

I gave my senior class speech with a sense of pride. I had survived this horrible experience of school and made it all the way through. But, of course, I also dropped in a few improvised sentences at the end, emploring the crowd to come to Jesus. After all, in my mind, God was the one who had given me favor and gotten me through it all. I was also aware that Pastor Joe was in the crowd (along with other congregants) and wanted to make them proud.

Onward and Upward

My high school Christian experience cemented my belief in the church. If I'd risen from the ashes of such tumultuous teenage years, I thought I could be victorious in anything. Where the Republican Party had been a bridge between my dad and me, the Christian faith became a lifesaver to the darkest part of myself. If I could live this "new creation" and detest the "old nature," I could find life and love in everything I did.

My final summer at home reminded me of the adventure ahead of me. I was cautiously optimistic about moving away to college, not knowing what was in store. I'd built a name for myself in my community and felt at home in the church. In a way, I felt closer to the congregants than my own blood family. I contemplated staying in the area not to leave them but knew I needed to get out of a town with so many reminders of early traumas.

I feared that in college I'd be tempted by my independence and "fall away" (a term for believers who fall away from the faith). So I constantly had my Bible study group pray over me as I set out into this new phase. I thought I'd always be grounded in my faith, which is why shortly after I turned 18, I got a tattoo on my inner bicep in Hebrew that read: "Jesus my King."

I later found out my tattoo was grammatically incorrect — it mixed old and modern Hebrew. I'd taken the inscription from the college group camp shirt and trusted its credibility. I justified the tattoo by saying it represented my old self and new self — a clever justification if ever there were one. As seems to be the theme of my Christian life, I have since covered that mistake.

THOUGHT: HOMOSEXUALITY

On a quest to come to some sort of reconciliation between my feelings and my faith, I made a last-ditch effort to research the premise of homosexuality in the Bible towards the end of my Christian life. This quest started about a year before I left the faith entirely.

With enough Bible college classes under my belt to have earned a bachelor's in Biblical studies (possibly even a master's degree), I thought I had the bandwidth to do a deep dive about homosexuality and the Bible. Keep in mind that I'm now several years removed from this era and have since worked extensively to purge my brain of this information. This is my recollection of what took place and the information I seemed to retain.

Opening Up

Before exploring what the Bible had to say on the subject of homosexuality, I intentionally avoided more liberal-leaning doctrinal beliefs. I rebuked anything that didn't align with the belief that homosexuality was an abomination (this was born of a deep-seated fear of sliding down the slippery slope to one day accepting my sexuality). When faced with liberal beliefs, I refuted them as misinformed understandings of proper biblical interpretation, often even questioning the faith of the one who believed in such doctrine.

Resolved to find the truth, I tried to cast aside my prejudice towards liberal theologians. I may have been questioning the church's beliefs on homosexuality, but my conservativism was still in full force. Exploring anything outside of that was a scary prospect that would pull on a personal thread I wasn't yet ready to unravel.

My first stop was a tip I got from a housemate, telling me that the pastor of Real Life's sister church in the heart of the Castro in San Francisco had recently spoken about homosexuality and the proper biblical response by Christians. Their church was relatively new and coming to grips with their identity in the community. After receiving some not-so-favorable feedback from the gay community, the pastor made it his mission to understand homosexuality and the

Bible. I learned of this and heard a recording from a sermon he'd given on the subject. It was clear by listening to the sermon that the pastor humbly presented this subject after a soul-searching moment.

His community's response clearly affected him, feeling a conviction to represent his faith with the best of care. Should he venture too far to the left, he'd risk being labeled a blasphemous teacher and relegated to the list of other liberal theologians who were supposedly destined for hell for their false teachings. He was not yet ready to accept homosexuality on a broader scale. Still, he *questioned* the premise of condemnation held so firmly in the Evangelical belief system — a system that hit hard when passing judgment on the wider Christian community.

He had done his homework, digging up exegeses material (material critical of scriptures) as well as providing historical context. "Context" was a fancy term thrown around by most Christians whenever anyone challenged the faith; it prompted the opponent to put the verse back into its original meaning and intent. However, the *context* was rarely a matter of concern for firmly held beliefs about certain sins in the church, like homosexuality.

This pastor brought context to the writings in Romans, talking about how "men exchanged the natural use of the woman, burning in lust for one another." This passage was foundational to my beliefs about the *sin* of homosexuality.

It was the only passage of text that explicitly outlined homosexual behavior — painting the image of real homosexual acts. This passage was the cornerstone of my firmly held beliefs that I would one day be cured of this wretched sin, for it outlined the natural use of heterosexuality being exchanged for lust towards one of the same-sex. To me, it was clear at face value that this passage explained homosexuality as a choice, not a lifestyle. Further understanding of the cultural context taught in this sermon illuminated my short-sighted beliefs.

Roman Homosexuality

In the book of Romans, Paul addresses the Roman people. While Christianity eventually became dominant (thanks to emperor Constantine paving the way to make it the Empire's official religion by way of his own conversion to Christianity), Roman Christians were persecuted for their faith for a long time. Paul thus saw it as his duty to encourage the Roman people to stay steadfast, true to the faith. He was afraid of them falling back into their old Roman ways and renouncing their faith.

There were plenty of behaviors adopted in Roman culture that were seen as detestable in the Christian faith and a threat to Roman Christians. A Roman person who adopted Christianity as their religion not only faced persecution for their faith (including likely execution) but had to forsake customs common to their culture and community. One of these is addressed in the first chapter of the book of Romans, and it pertains to sexual sin.

In those times, it was common for heterosexual couples to have homosexual sex outside the confines of their marriage. Ancient historians have uncovered ancient text and illustrations that explicitly depict heterosexual men taking "effeminate" men and conquering them by penetration or even having sexual relations with male slaves. This was a commonly practiced tradition of homosexual *rape*.

Ancient Roman's idea of homosexuality was *far* removed from the concept of monogamous, committed homosexual relationships that we see today. To the straight ancient Roman man who partook in such acts, his homosexuality was all about conquest, not commitment or care for the other person. In Paul's rebuke of such practices, it is believed that he outlined the context of what was taking place: women and men were exchanging the natural use of their heterosexual unions to burn in lust for one another.

These were *heterosexual* married people committed to having sex for procreation with one another, who then committed adultery by turning to same-sex counterparts for sexual pleasure and/or conquest. Although Paul describes homosexual acts in this passage, an alternative interpretation (and frankly, with greater contextual sensitivity) to the Evangelical understanding is that Paul addressed the sin of adultery and rape, *not* homosexuality.

The widely held interpretation of this passage by Evangelicals pertaining to homosexuality fails to consider this context. If this passage can be used to condemn all homosexuality, it would be reasonable to assume that other passages relating to heterosexual sins could be used to condemn heterosexual sex altogether — just as they do with this passage and homosexuality. The lack of contextual interpretation is a lazy and shortsighted adaptation by the church, which has resulted in the condemnation of many in the church who identify as homosexual.

Further, the word "homosexual" doesn't show up anywhere in the Scriptures (neither Old nor New Testament). In fact, the word "sodomy" was translated in the mid-twentieth century (yes, twentieth) as referring to homosexual activity only. Clearly, sodomy isn't exclusive to the homosexual community, as heterosexuals practice it. If it's "unlawful" to be homosexual, it should be just as unlawful to practice anal sex. Yet many Evangelical churches accept anal sex between consensual heterosexual married partners as a personal choice, not a sin. Context is critical.

Remember: heterosexual married men "[left] the natural use of the woman, burned in their lust for one another, men with men committing what is shameful...". Again, heterosexual married men turned to their wives for procreation, then turned to men for pleasure. Some heterosexual men even raped other men they deemed effeminate or slaves, penetrated them to manifest their conquest and prove their (toxic) masculinity. Considering the cultural context, it's safe to say that the bigger sin isn't monogamous, consensual homosexuality. Again, *context is critical.*

Hypocrisy in Interpretation

In my opinion, the problem isn't so much what is written in the Bible as beliefs about the Bible's authority itself. Evangelical Christians believe the Bible is the literal "Word of God" — that what is written in it is infallible, absolute truth, and ordained by God. To Evangelical Christians, it's not so much about interpreting the Bible to fit the Christian's lifestyle but interpreting the Christian's lifestyle to fit the Bible.

All this is to say that the Bible is a book that has had more than its fair share of human intervention, and it's therefore nearly impossible to assume it is indeed the "Word of God." Its complicated history includes murky authorship, multiple translations, and writings outlining events that sometimes occurred fifty to eighty years before their description (if at all). The power Evangelical Christians ascribe to the Bible doesn't square with its construction. And for a belief system to hold such strong convictions about matters that attack the identity of human beings, there should be equally strong evidence that God has indeed ordained this book as His final word to His people.

A classic example is when the writer of one of the books to the church of Corinth states:

"Now I commend you because you remember me in everything and maintain the traditions even as I delivered them to you. But I want you to understand that the head of every man is Christ, the head of a wife is her husband, and the head of Christ is God. Every man who prays or prophesies with his head covered dishonors his head, but every wife who prays or prophesies with her head uncovered dishonors her head, since it is the same as if her head were shaven. For if a wife will not cover her head, then she should cut her hair short.

But since it is disgraceful for a wife to cut off her hair or shave her head, let her cover her head. For a man ought not to cover his head, since he is the image and glory of God, but woman is the glory of man. For man was not made from woman, but woman from man. Neither was man created for woman, but woman for man. That is why a wife ought to have a symbol of authority on her head, because of the angels."

- 1 Corinthians 11:2-10

There are plenty of problematic messages in this text, focusing on just one – wives being required to cover their heads while in church (among being submissive and treated as lesser to their husbands, women lesser than men). Most Evangelicals have interpreted the passage requiring women to wear head shawls in church being a culturally outdated mandate, stating that considering the context of it being a cultural norm of the time in the Church of Corinth. However, the same contextual epiphanies haven't been included in some of the most horrendously misinterpreted scriptures, like those supposedly related to homosexuality.

The perspective of homosexuality in Evangelical churches has been to denounce it as sin primarily based on Paul's book to the Romans, but this doesn't consider cultural context at all. When one looks at what was happening in Rome at the time, it makes sense that Paul was addressing adultery between heterosexual, monogamous couples. Somehow this context has been overlooked as the Evangelical church "burns in lust" to eradicate homosexuality. I can't say it enough: context is critical. This type of hypocrisy and carelessness was one of *many* reasons why I ultimately chose to leave the faith altogether.

Jesus and Homosexuality

It's also important to note that Jesus, the source of worship in Christianity itself, *never* spoke about homosexuality or sodomy. He had plenty of sins to condemn — most notably (and ironically) the hypocrisy of the religious. Jesus' condemnation came down on religious leaders of the time (the Pharisees) who he once called, among other sassy things, "white-washed tombs." He literally said *to them* that they might have looked great on the outside but were dead on the inside—the literal definition of a mic-drop.

In fact, "homosexuality" wasn't even remotely addressed in the Christian faith until Paul made it his life's mission to spread the "good news of salvation through Jesus." His mission, it's worth noting, sprang from a personal experience of being blinded by God after persecuting Christians. It's ironic that a religion was even created in Jesus' name when Jesus had such disdain for religion.

Given who Jesus was and what he preached, as outlined in the first four books of the New Testament (also known as the Gospels – the teachings and words of Jesus, supposedly written by those who claimed to be "eye-witnesses" of Jesus), I think he would be appalled by what was then attributed to him within the other 23 books that make up the New Testament. When the New Testament was canonized sometime in the *fifth* century (long after Jesus' death), there was a lot of debate about which books should be included in the Bible and excluded. Centuries later, the final decision was made on which books would remain. In the sixteenth century, during the Protestant Reformation, the books that made up the Apocrypha were removed (this is the primary difference between Catholics and Protestants).

Arguably (and for the sake of time), the current New Testament consists of four sections: The Gospels, the Acts of the Apostles, the Epistles, and the Great Revelation. The Gospels, as mentioned earlier, are testimonies of those who claim to have had the first-hand experience with Jesus. They account for the words of Jesus, written decades after he had died and supposedly risen from the dead (one of the books of the Gospels is believed to have been written over 100 years after Jesus' death. How he lived to remember/ write it down, God only knows). They are the *only* Biblical accounts of Jesus' actual words, written by (supposedly) three of the four original disciples of Jesus. These are the Biblical accounts that recount Jesus' actual words, accounting for the "gospel of Jesus" (literally, the "good news of Jesus").

The Acts of the Apostles details the calling of his followers to spread the gospel and their subsequent quest to do so (it also outlines Paul's conversion to Christianity). The Epistles detail very specific rules of the faith and are seen as the source of doctrinal beliefs held today. The book of Romans is considered one of the books of the Epistles. The Book of Revelation is a single book detailing the prophecy of the Final Days/Judgement Day, the time when Jesus will supposedly return for his "elect," leaving the rest of us to experience Judgement Day to later burn in hell for all eternity.

All 27 of these books were written primarily by Paul (13 of 27 books), disciples, or those who claimed to have some sort of authority from God to write them. Many of the authors were questionable, meaning they were not actually identified in the writing of the books, so it is only assumed who wrote which books. The decision to include those books in the final canonized Bible was strictly a theological test: that they must have aligned with the general doctrinal statements of the other books they chose. All this to say - a curious and complicated origin for such a powerful book.

I will let you draw your own conclusion.

PART

2

COLLEGE YEARS

BROKEBACK BUNKHOUSE

Moving away to college was my first taste of true free-dom. As I'd been accepted to several Bible colleges but de-nied state leadership in the FFA, I decided I needed to get out of town and start over.

I hadn't seriously considered community college until I lost the FFA state leadership opportunity. My original plan had been to leverage experience in that role to get a full-ride scholarship to a four-year school of my choice (and, of course, continue to spread the gospel of Jesus). It turned out I was number 13 out of the 12 they selected, which stung. And apparently, my extreme religious beliefs had been a concern. It was also painful that one of my best friends in regional leadership *did* win a state leadership po-sition (I was proud of him and needed time to recover).

We'd talked about attending the same college and staying friends forever, so my loss felt even more profound. After licking my wounds over that defeat, I came to terms with the fact that my family couldn't afford a private Christian school; community college seemed like the only option. However, I wasn't willing to go to college in my hometown to fear running into my former classmates, so I set out for central California.

I had friends in that region — a group I'd met while serving in regional FFA leadership. They'd spoken of a community college in their area that was known to be a feeder school to four-year universities; its national reputation as a top school meant you were practically a shoo-in for wherever you wanted to transfer to after completion. It was also well-known for its party scene.

Deep down, I knew college would be a period of rediscovery for me, though I wasn't vocal about this with church friends for fear of being misinterpreted and judged. I expected college to be fun and knew I needed to let my hair down a bit. The truth was, I was pretty rigid, and holding onto a worldview of absolute truth seemed too constricting as I set out on my journey of independence. This was especially true when suddenly being surrounded by people from all different kinds of cultural backgrounds. It was all good in word to remain rooted in my faith during this new season of life, but I felt an inkling to loosen up a bit — to be free to explore.

On My Own

I was assigned to private, off-campus housing. As soon as I knew where I'd be living, I stuffed my Jeep Cherokee with my possessions and headed to central California. I felt the freedom instantly, thinking about everything I wanted to do, like buy my own groceries without worrying about how healthy they were! Even paying my own bills sounded fun (lucky for me, these were subsidized by my parents — a thank you for choosing a government-funded community college over a private Christian school). Though I didn't *have* to get a job while in school, the work ethic instilled in me at a very young age had me feel duty-bound to find some sort of work, whether seasonal or part-time. So as soon I got settled, I made it my priority to look for work.

I took in my first semester with caution. I'd landed a part-time gig at a deli in town and was desperately looking to plug myself into a church. Unfortunately, I was unsuccessful in that endeavor, as I found it hard to connect with a specific church group. Some churches were too relaxed, while others felt like I had to wear a three-piece suit just to fit in. It was overwhelming, especially after the disappointment of not clicking at the sister church of my home church in the area.

I chalked it up to "the Spirit not leading me anywhere" and "God will provide in his perfect timing" — clichéd

Christian phrases to ease the ego. However, my independence was calling deep down, making it just fine that I
hadn't yet found a church to call home.

Cowboy Down

What I lacked in holiness, I made up for in drunkenness.
I had fun and went into (what the church would deem) a
fallback. The pleasure of college outweighed the stringent
lifestyle of a strict Christian — a fact first witnessed by my
housemates. Although my actions resembled a more relaxed version of myself, I still held to the principles of my
faith in word. My strong beliefs defied the actions of my
housemates, calling me out on certain contradictions. I was
a rigid bore to be around when I wasn't drunk.

Due to my hypocritical rigidity, I eventually became a
social outcast, so I reached out to the group of friends that
were my motivation for moving to the town in the first
place. They knew me from my high school days, and I felt
they accepted my awkwardness. They were cowboys who
lived in the backwoods and worked on ranches. They too
partook in evil and sin but under the open air of the countryside.

They understood I was religious but had space for me
since they were raised in strict Catholic households. They

also practiced some sort of religion outside of their shenanigans. I secretly looked up to them for their ability to reconcile their faith with their antics, despite my Evangelical beliefs that questioned their salvation. They constantly talked about parties and girls they had fun with in high school, bragging about their ability to get alcohol as minors. During my first semester in college, I reunited with them after the tragic death of one of our mutual friends: Colin.

The tragedy struck deep. Colin (who I'd known through FFA leadership) had been killed in a devastating car crash. I was invited to meet at his parents' house after his death. I'd met his parents a few times when we were in leadership together, so it wasn't strange to see them; what was weird was witnessing the new void in their lives.

We sat together, and they cried as they planned for the funeral. I made myself available for whatever they needed — to pick up food, lend a listening ear, or just witness their suffering. Looking into both his parent's and sister's faces, the pain I felt was difficult, but nothing like losing a son or a brother. However, a tremendous burden was when Brad entered the room — dead-faced and still in shock.

Brad was defeated. He'd lost both Colin and another friend in the accident when they were driving home from a night of partying. To this day, I'm unsure of the exact details of that night, but I do remember hearing that Brad had decided to go in a different car, ahead of them, to meet up at one of their houses. That night, only Brad made it home safely.

Brad and Colin were best friends. They both served in regional leadership and were constantly mistaken for brothers — not because they looked alike, but because they were inseparable. Many believed Brad only ran for regional office so he could be with Colin. Their friendship had been forged early on in life (along with the other friend killed that night). After losing both, Brad spiraled out of control. Friends around him constantly questioned his stability and whereabouts. I felt the need to step in to console him, which, much to my surprise and pleasure, led to a much more committed friendship than I originally anticipated.

I felt like I didn't know how to be a real friend. All my friends had either left me, or I'd left them. Friendships I'd made in the church were conditional (a theme I came to realize after removing myself from the faith): the "fellowship" we shared went only as far as the community. Moving to a new area separated me from my old community, and I knew I had to start over again — to prove myself worthy of the faith before that church body would accept me as one of their own.

When I went home for breaks, Real Life church embraced me, but I was no longer a part of their lives — so there was always a kind of separation. No longer did I know them intimately through Bible study, prayer requests, or church gatherings. Community in the church meant sharing the same faith and also being an active member of that community. Faith alone didn't bring about fellowship; active participation welded bonds.

And where the church rejected me, Brad and his cowboy friends embraced me.

Beginning of Brotherhood

Before Colin's death, I'd never personally experienced tragedy, and I was grounded in a belief system that only took me as far as clichéd theological phrases and verses. In times of crisis, the church relied on trite phrases like, *God will make you stronger from this*, *have faith*, and *praise the Lord* — what I'd later term verbal masturbation.

I found myself in a delicate situation; I attempted to be the best friend I could to a deeply wounded individual. It started slow — I'd show up to Brad's parents' house to hang out with his little siblings and chat with his parents after the dust settled from the tragedy. I thought being present was the first step to friendship — showing Brad that I cared about him enough to meet him where he was in his devastation.

I thoroughly loved my time with Brad's family; it gave me a glimpse into what a caring, compassionate, and loving family looked like. I found myself driving up to his parents' house on days I didn't have school or work, just to hang out with his mom and the kids while his dad was away at work. She shared her insights on motherhood with me, which made me jealous, and I wished my family situation were different.

My mom was a caring person but very rough around the edges. I don't remember her cradling me when I was scared or sad — I just remember her rage at my antics. My relationship with her was complex. I knew she cared deeply for me, but her past traumas mixed with her strict cultural upbringing in Middle Eastern Catholicism strained our relationship. I learned to fear her at an early age. Being the mischievous one, I was constantly the subject of her short temper and frustration.

Her own experience in Catholic school nurtured her insecurities and famous form of punishment. She was constantly the brunt of her teacher's aggressions with a ruler to the back of the hand for "not being smart enough." She adopted this form of punishment as her own, knowing from experience that it was effective. Her insecurity concerning her academic shortcomings was made known to me by her sister shortly before my mom's passing. It was common for people to pick on my mom for her distant personality as a child. Her trauma made sense when she lashed out at someone who didn't understand what she was saying due to her heavy accent.

My grandma on my dad's side was the opposite of my mom. She was abandoned in Lebanon during the Great Depression with two of her younger sisters, and she was left responsible for taking care of them. Her parents moved the rest of her family to the United States to provide a better life. When my grandma eventually came over to the States, she carried the weight of her traumas after the death of one of her sisters while they were stranded in Lebanon. However, her experience made her an independent force, evident in her attempted escape from an arranged marriage to a man with no emotional connection. She wasn't successful in avoiding the union as she was discovered and forced to enter "holy" matrimony.

My grandma resented her husband, and for many good reasons. I never knew my grandpa, but from her and my father's siblings' stories, he was a complex man with "old country" beliefs about family. Being the man of the house, he ruled with an iron fist. My grandma began to resent him more for his wandering ways, so his passing was nothing but a celebration of liberation for her. She dove into social events and clubs, becoming Miss Santa Barbara for her work in the community. No matter where she went, everyone knew her. She was the unofficial mayor and self-proclaimed queen of the town. Her personality flourished as she pioneered her own life, which was what drew me to her most.

My grandma was kind and compassionate, and she literally "worshiped the ground I walked on" (a phrase she often said to me), which was the opposite of my experience with my parents. After deciding to spend as much time with my grandma after my first sleepover in elementary school, I began to distance myself from my mom. At the time, I didn't understand the effect this had on my mom until I was an adult. She resented my grandma for "taking me away from her," making our relationship more complex.

Every person my mom encountered seemed always to misunderstand her. Being rough on the edges, people found her intimidating...especially me. She sacrificed everything in her mid-thirties to assimilate to a country she found strange so she could start a family. She didn't even speak the language until she took classes after her marriage to my dad. She constantly said critical things about American culture, and being born and raised in the States, I couldn't relate.

However, she found ways to show her affection: providing her family with a clean & warm home, having dinner ready every night, applying her cultural potions and lotions to heal our illnesses, and sneaking in R-rated movies for my siblings and me to watch with her during the nights my father attended to his commitments to the Masonic

Temple. She tried her best to provide for her family, even though she was dealt an unfair hand in life. Being treated like "runt of the litter" by her siblings, she formed an insufficiency complex. Again, she sacrificed everything for her family with the cards she'd been dealt, a reality I didn't come to appreciate until it was too late - a theme I made sure to hit home in her eulogy.

* * *

Back to Brad's family. His mom was warm, welcoming, and extremely humble. She constantly expressed grief for her eldest child, who was experiencing a huge loss. I was drawn to her qualities of motherhood and formed a bond with her like a pseudo-mother.

His dad was also outstanding – a salt-of-the-earth kind of guy in touch with his feelings and emotions. He was a true God-fearing Catholic man with a temper that flared when triggered but rooted in a heart of gold. He and his family were a devout religious bunch and demonstrated the acts of their faith better than any family I knew. They weren't like the Catholics I'd learned about in church.

Most Evangelicals believe the Catholic faith is filled with idolatry and that believers of that denomination aren't truly saved like the rest of Christians because of their worship of saints. That didn't stop me from coming along when Brad's family invited me to church services and to take part in communion. Their family lived out their faith better than any Christian I knew at the time and show-cased what a perfectly imperfect family could look like. Partaking in their religious practices was a conflict I was willing to wrestle with to understand better.

Cowboy Up

Occasionally, after hanging out with Brad's family, I stayed for after-parties, when Brad and his buddies would gather around a backyard bonfire and drink their brains out. These nights were magical — like none I'd ever experienced. If sunset had a scent, it would be the smell of back-woods. There was something mystical about those late fall/ early winter nights. A feeling not often recognized at the moment but pondered upon some years later. There was a bit of nostalgia in the smell of the creosote while driving through rural land with the windows down, heater roaring, and music blasting.

Even more powerful was the sense of community and belonging that formed when his friends came over. It was a group of imperfect people coming together to share and enjoy each other's company. Yes, they drank and made fun of each other, but they also maintained a deep bond and connection that often went deeper than blood. They understood each other in a way that transcended judgment or criticism; they accepted each other for who they were, not who they were trying to be. Their differences united them, not separated them.

Here was a community I found even more attractive than the church because it seemed authentic and tangible. Their differences were their strength, united by the loyalty to help each other out in times of need. It was the kind of community I desired more than anything. Drawn to this crowd, I decided to stay and observe. Eventually, being the hollowed-out, impressionable person I was, I joined in on their antics, occasionally being the brunt of their fun.

One night, after knocking back a few shots of Jager and consuming an entire can of Copenhagen snuff, I let them practice their roping skills on me. They pretended I was a calf, having me run around while they lassoed me into submission. I thought it was fun even though they yelled things at me like "sand n***er" and "dune c**n" because of my Middle Eastern descent, and inflicted permanent scars on my elbows and back (from being dragged by the ropes). As the new guy in the group, I had no problem with this informal initiation. To me, it was good fun – I felt like I was part of something. I was invincible. I thought I belonged with these cowboys because I mattered.

The whole experience was enchanting — we were out in the open country air, drinking until we puked and talked about pointless shit. I'd never felt freer in my life. There was such a carefree nature about it; I felt like I had a new life. There were days when I felt on top of the world, especially when I popped a couple of opioids and drove around country roads. Once the opioids kicked in, I didn't have a care in the world.

Redneck Antics & Addiction

Brad eventually moved out of his parent's place; onto the property of a woman he'd met who needed work done. She owned a few acres of land that included a barn full of horses. She needed a full-time rancher to help her around her estate. Her house, a mansion on a hill, was surrounded by rolling hills in the middle of nowhere. It was unclear what her husband did for work, but it was evident that he was extremely successful. She never had to work but quickly busted out rolls of cash to pay Brad (while drinking wine and nursing her dogs as if they were her children). She offered Brad the studio over the barn, which became the new place for our antics.

I worked at Starbucks at the time, and Brad occasionally called to ask what I was doing that night. In exchange for a Caramel Frappuccino, he'd pick me up after work in his truck and take me to his neck of the woods, where we'd meet up with the guys and drink. In the dark place of grief, he found a new light of hope — a friendship with someone he was familiar with but who wasn't tied to his environment of pain. I, too, felt a sense of newness. I felt loved and included. For the first time in my life, I felt like I was seen. And wanted.

One night after excessive drinking, someone had the bright idea of tying twine around some compressed fencing Brad had taken down earlier that day and attaching it to the back of an ATV. We rode on it, calling it "redneck inner tubing." It was eventually my turn, and they were relentless at trying to throw me off. Finally, after a few turns and bumps, I got my grip. The stakes were high, so whoever was driving laid on the gas and watched me in amusement.

Eventually, the fencing hit a dip, and I was thrown off when my foot got caught between the fencing and the drop. I felt the sting of pain, but it was nothing alcohol, and chewing tobacco couldn't fix. So we partied on, and it wasn't until the next day that I went to the hospital. It turned out my foot was broken, and I needed a boot. Starbucks didn't want me back at work until I was well. Seemingly unemployed and with a new group of friends, I casually looked for other work while enjoying my time at the ranch after school.

This is the time that my opioid addiction took on legs. I was given a prescription for Vicodin to ease the pain of my broken foot. The feeling was sensational, dangerously coupled with alcohol at times. I became a master at getting my doctor to prescribe me more, finding ways to lie about my pain. Struggling with a loss of identity, I found purpose in feeling on top of the world. I felt more open, more willing to allow others into my life. But when the buzz wore off, I was back to my anxiety-ridden existence. Opioids gave me a carefree feeling and I couldn't get enough.

My struggle with this addiction has ebbed and flowed throughout my life. When I felt my lowest, I would turn to this stimulant to shed momentary light on my world of darkness. It became a familiar crutch to escape the pain of my depression and anxiety. Being on opioids gave me a release like no other. What I couldn't control in my life, opioids gave me the peace in not caring so much.

After losing my mom to her many ailments, I turned to this substance for comfort. I remember the weightless, careless feeling I felt once they started to get their hold. It was as if nothing mattered; all the cares of this life seemed to diminish as I sunk into a feeling of ecstasy. Whether dealing with my complicated feelings concerning my mom or the wild depression I felt being in a job that felt monotonous, opioids gave me an out for a moment in time. I could feel the numbness first in my face, down to my body, and eventually to my feelings.

Today, my reliance on this hallucinogen has been much suppressed with the introduction of SSRIs. There are still moments that I am tempted to rely on my resources, but with the tools I have been given through therapy and energy work, along with the SSRI I am currently on, this temptation is significantly suppressed.

Brokeback Bunkhouse

My roommates started getting suspicious of my whereabouts. I rarely slept at home, and when I did return, it was just to shower and grab a change of clothes since I was heading back up to the ranch to be with the guys.

I was having the time of my life. The only time I went to the city was to go to class, work, or pick up supplies for the ranch. Since I wasn't having much luck finding another job and spent so much time at the ranch, I began helping Brad out; he took me under his wing to teach me how to be a ranch hand.

When I wasn't working, I was at the main house. The owner and I became close as she shared some juicier stories about her life and husband. I always seemed to make friends with older women, as I was comfortable sharing my emotions. Women seemed caring and nurturing yet strong and opinionated, unlike men's gruff, cold demeanor. It also helped that I wasn't sexually attracted to women, so my walls went down quicker. I found women's personalities more calming, and this woman seemed to recognize my ease in conversation as she started to leverage our friendship for her benefit.

It soon became apparent that she was a narcissist — she constantly talked about herself positively and didn't take well to critical feedback. She shared numerous stories about how people had done her wrong and how she was the hero in every story. Unlike Brad's mom, she was blind to her shortcomings and feared many things in life. She was extremely paranoid and constantly prodded me to tell her what was going on down in what she called the *Brokeback Bunkhouse*.

But even with her erratic behavior, I somehow felt comfortable, given her openness and perceived vulnerability. Little did I know she was using me to get information on Brad. I was young and dumb and didn't see the signs. It was as if she had romantic feelings for him. And who could blame her? Brad was absolutely stunning and kindhearted.

Brad was the group player; he had dark blue eyes you could gaze into forever, and through which you could sometimes catch a glimpse of his soul. With blond hair and the body of a hard-working cowboy, his charm could make you lose your religion. He was quite the ladies' man, known for his playboy antics. He had a confidence about him that was enticing and yet humble at the same time. I found myself having feelings for him but suppressed them on account of — you know, being a *gay cowboy*? It was ludicrous. I couldn't imagine it ever happening, but I also couldn't imagine life without Brad in it.

Living the Dream

I tried to transfer to a Starbucks closer to the ranch but was denied and ultimately terminated. Since I'd been helping more at the ranch and he knew I was far from home, Brad offered another guy and me the chance to live with him in the studio apartment above the barn in exchange for helping him around the ranch.

I didn't even hesitate, immediately informing my roommates of the change. But, unfortunately, I was locked into a one-year lease that I tried desperately to get out of, to no avail. So I just paid my portion of the rent even though I didn't live there, and I didn't care – I was living the dream.

Living in the Brokeback Bunkhouse was a dream I wished lasted longer than the few short months it did. I'd fantasized about this life — being a cowboy renegade living in the country with my "buddy." But I constantly had to check myself for letting my homosexual feelings get the best of me. Since Brad was always seeing different women, I fantasized about what it would be like to be his fling — imagining how kind and compassionate he would be, yet at the same time forceful and passionate. But, of course, I couldn't imagine what these women felt; I was always jealous of the girls he brought home.

These feelings welled up deep inside me, sometimes manifesting in "protest behavior," like avoidance or passive aggression. Unfortunately, I knew I could never express my feelings or admit them to anyone since I'd risk retaliation and rejection. Being gay in this environment was taboo. Much like the church, if I wanted to continue to be a member of my newfound community, I had to reject my homosexual feelings. Finally, I was accepted into a new life. I didn't want to fuck up, but I can't say there weren't times I tried to push the envelope.

One time, while Brad was taking a shower, my other roommate and I decided to mess with him. The bathroom door didn't lock, and we started turning on the water in the sink, so his shower water came out cold. Then we upped our game by filling cups with ice-cold water and sneaking into the bathroom to dump them on him over the top of the shower. Brad threatened to come out naked and beat us senseless. I imagined what that would be like — seeing him naked. I tested faith in that challenge while the other roommate retreated outside to attend to the work at hand for the day. I filled up one last cup of water and made a final plunge over the shower curtain. He sprang out of the shower to tackle me to the ground. I felt a sense of magnificent exhilaration ... and knew it wasn't mutual.

Beginning of the End

Eventually, the dream died. The lady on the hill became more toxic and volatile than I could have imagined. The familiar story she'd once shared intimately with me about how others wronged her was turned on us; she fabricated stories about how we were doing her wrong, saying we were stealing from her. It felt like she was going insane — like she was suffering from an extreme case of bipolar disorder. Her personality seemed to flicker on and off like a light switch. Brad and I started getting frantic, belligerent voicemails and letters from her, with threats that she'd sue us all. When she finally kicked us out of the Brokeback Bunkhouse, we were *all* out of a job.

Brad moved back into his parent's house while the other roommate and I returned to our original living situations. I felt defeated moving back to my apartment, but one of my housemates couldn't have been more accepting and loving. I was now glad I hadn't broken my lease; I would've been homeless.

Things never seemed to be the same between Brad and me after that. I could feel his distance and felt wildly responsible for how things had gone down. There was no indication that I'd done anything wrong, but as was my custom, I took the blame. I felt a deep sense of shame just for being me, so I found myself the subject of my own ridicule, no matter the circumstances. I hated who I was, so whatever bad went on around me seemed to be my own doing. It was as if I believed my very existence manifested terrible things.

What I feared most was becoming a reality: I was losing Brad. My fear got the best of me as I made erratic decisions; I'd send him texts that would trigger some sort of emotional response, then pretend I'd meant to send it to someone else. I gave up everything when he made himself available to me, canceling plans with anyone if he wanted to hang out. I was losing myself trying to keep this friendship alive and annoyed whenever he went silent, questioning whether he wanted to be my friend anymore.

I didn't, of course, consider his perspective. I didn't recognize the insurmountable loss he had experienced, to then be kicked to the curb again by losing his job and suffering the humiliation of needing to move back into his parents' house. I only saw my pain. I felt rejected by his retreat, which triggered feelings in me that made me internally erratic. Ultimately the intensity became too much, as the feelings of rejection provoked in me a familiar reaction:

to reject someone else before they rejected me. I knew I had to *leave* before *being left*, so I sent one final text that ended it all.

After being kicked out of the Brokeback Bunkhouse, there were plenty of items that were too burdensome for Brad to store at his parents' house. I asked my sister if it would be ok to keep some of the stuff at her house, knowing she had ample room, and having his things allowed me to hold on to Brad a bit longer. When he asked me to deliver the stored items, I responded with an emotionally charged response, telling him that he would have to come to get them himself if he wanted his things. This was my final attempt to see him in person after he became more distant. That didn't comb over well for Brad as he begrudgingly drove down in his pickup truck. We hardly spoke to each other - offering to help him load it up but profusely refusing. As he slammed the door and hit the gas, I knew that I had lost him forever.

Starting Over, Again

Things got crazy – or at least I felt like I'd gone crazy. Deflated, I focused on finishing my school semester to look for full-time work and find another place to live. I needed a new community of friends, whether from work or home. A housemate and I talked about getting an apartment together, but he seemed intimidated by my behavior (moving to the ranch for a time). Plus, another opportunity seemed more enticing.

I decided to move into a two-bedroom apartment with Justin, one of Brad's frenemies, to make Brad jealous. He and Justin were supposedly indifferent to each other, and Brad found it annoying that I decided to live with him. I made this decision on a whim, knowing it would get under Brad's skin, and I didn't care; I just wanted some rising out of Brad, which seemed to do the trick. Unfortunately, it worked a little too well, as it appeared to be the final nail in the coffin between us.

My time with Justin was difficult. I began to see why Brad didn't care for him; he was a hard-headed man set in his ways. I didn't care at first, as I had an ulterior motive in living with him, but it became one of the most challenging living situations I ever endured. He and I eventually found our groove as housemates, but I couldn't wait for our one-year lease to end. I made it through that year by partaking in antics with a new group of friends and didn't care that I'd burned yet another bridge when it came to housemates.

My days with Brad ended with a tragic sense of loss. I missed a friendship that had seemed unconditional and felt that my crazy obsessiveness in trying to keep him in my life had ruined our friendship. As I got older, I realized my attempts to keep him were a desperate attempt to keep a part of my identity intact. I hid behind this friend-ship, conforming to a pseudo-identity to fit in and belong. I didn't know my own needs and wants because I wasn't comfortable with who I was, so I created an identity out of my insecurities. What I needed and desired were in conflict: I needed a friend, but what I expected was a savior.

COMING TO JESUS, AGAIN

As much as I missed my days on the ranch, I was beginning to find a rhythm of my own. After landing a full-time job at a graphics design company, I decided to finish my community college classes at night. This worked out well; I had enough money to party my ass off while pursuing three associate degrees. When I wasn't working or attending school, I was at house parties or getting older friends to buy alcohol so that I could throw parties of my own at my sister's house. Waking up with a hangover became the regular — nothing coffee and tobacco couldn't fix.

My sister suffered the most from my recklessness and debauchery. A year younger than me in school, she had moved to the same area for college. By my second year of community college, I was a full-fledged member of the party scene. She inherited my old Jeep when I purchased a new truck and frequently used it to rescue me. She was always the sober one, saying she never really liked the taste of alcohol. I later wondered if that was just an excuse she used to keep an eye on me and be there in my times of need (which were plentiful). We loved each other deeply, but it was often a one-sided relationship during our college years, as she was always the one to come to my rescue.

Avoiding a DUI

When I was twenty years old and mere months away from obtaining the legal right to buy alcohol, one of the directors at work asked me to take care of her brother, who was visiting from Florida for the week. He was older (in his late 30s) but still had a taste for partying, so to appease my boss and have some fun of my own, I invited him over for a small house party with some friends from work. He hit it off with one of the girls his age, and they wanted to go clubbing that night.

I ended up taking six shots of Jose Cuervo within 5 minutes before jumping into my truck to go to a bar outside town with a notorious reputation for allowing minors. Unfortunately, good old Jose had kicked in by the time we got to the bar; I was a blacked-out mess. It's a wonder they let me into the club at all. To this day, the smell of tequila reminds me of this dreadful night.

For the rest of the night, the only thing I remember was being on the dance floor with a group of girls, dancing my ass off. The next thing I knew, bright red and blue lights flashed - cops had pulled us over for a busted taillight just three blocks away from my apartment. I was blacked out in the passenger seat. My boss's brother was at the wheel and, when breathalyzed, blew well above the limit. Miraculously, the police cut a deal with us: If we could get someone to pick us up, they'd let us go with a fix-it ticket.

I don't remember calling my sister, but I'll never forget the look on her face when she showed up. Talk about a sobering moment. I much preferred the flashing lights of the officer's vehicle to the ominously familiar headlights of her Jeep. She was first concerned, then furious with me. How could I blame her? This was one of the biggest mistakes of my life. Before letting me go, one of the officers wanted to test my drinking level — I remember him saying, "just for fun." He laughed in shock at the readout but didn't tell me my number. It too was well over the limit - and higher than the driver's results. Thank God I hadn't been the one who'd decided to drive that night.

My sister was silent as she drove both the driver to his hotel and me home. I tried to apologize, but she wasn't having any of it — she wanted me to be quiet. I couldn't blame her; I must have smelled like a liquor store after a massive earthquake. I knew this incident was a big deal and marked where my drinking had become a problem. I woke the next day to a blistering hangover that any stimulant couldn't cure. More painful was the need for some serious contemplation about what to do about my behavior.

Drunken Mess

My close encounter with a DUI didn't seem to deter me from drinking for long. And despite the carnage, my faith seemed always to take up some space in my life. In this season of my life, it looked like a nagging sense of obligation to a God who had given me a reprieve from a lifestyle I was terrified to pursue. I tucked these feelings away in my drunkenness while a sense of guilt and shame occasionally washed over me the following day. Drinking more than my body could handle became a regular occurrence, as I wanted so badly to drown out the voices in my head. I also wanted to impress my new friends.

When drunk, I felt on top of the world, then slept next to the devil in an abyss of hell the following day. I'd replay what I could remember from the night before, beating myself up for stupid things I'd said or done. I was ashamed of myself — the very essence of who I was — and it didn't help that my worldview was tied to a judgmental creator who was embarrassed by my existence when He saw what I was getting into.

This monkey on my back was also my closest friend. Getting drunk made me feel weightless and free. I once admitted to a group of friends that alcohol made me feel like I was experiencing my true self. When I drank, my walls came down, and I was a more caring, loving individual. Often the life of the party, I brought people together, expressed admiration for them, and got up on tables to dance while everyone cheered. My friends laughed at the sentiment that I found myself when I was drunk but didn't know the roots of these feelings.

My community always seemed to be in a state of transition, even as I desired nothing more than to fit in somewhere. After losing my home church community and then the cowboy community, I was desperate to find a place where I belonged. Alcohol helped me feel past my fears and experiment with different groups of people. It broke down barriers between social classes. I could be in a room full of people from wildly different backgrounds and upbringings, but intoxication united us. I wanted more of this openness and freedom in my life.

Despite all this newfound freedom, there were two topics of discussion I kept locked away, regardless of how drunk I got: Christianity and homosexuality. I frequently diverted questions about the foreign language tattoo under my arm, which made me feel guilty for what it revealed about my former life. I often thought about Bible verses that called Christians "ambassadors for Christ" — how could I do that when I was downing a shot, yelling pro-fanities, and dipping tobacco? (Yes, chewing tobacco was a thing for a few years of my life. To this day, I cringe when I think about it). I also often felt afraid of being condemned to hell for my behavior.

But nothing triggered me more than my thoughts of homosexuality.

Acting Out of the Closet

I casually dated women but never really found solace outside of platonic relationships with them. Meanwhile, my desire for men welled inside me, but I constantly refused to act on it. Eventually, on two occasions, I did act on my homosexuality (both very brief). However, on both occasions, I instantly experienced a tremendous sense of guilt and shame.

On one of these occasions, I visited home after discovering my grandma was in the hospital for what would be her last days on earth. Trying to escape the emotions of her inevitable death, I found myself at an adult bookstore known for its video collection. Little did I know there was an area in the back where you could watch videos, with holes cut out at crotch height that revealed the booth next door. I peeked my head into this space, curious yet hesitant. My rationale to myself was that I'd just go in once, hope to see a movie quickly, and be gone.

When I entered the booth, I noticed two shadowy figures, their attention on me. I peeked out from behind the curtain to see a man beaconing me to him. I ducked back in, afraid he'd seen me. A few minutes later, I discovered the intended purpose of those holes. My curiosity got the best of me, and I partook for about thirty seconds — then felt an overwhelming rush of shame. I got myself together and made a beeline for the door, not looking back.

When I got into my truck, I started yelling at myself, "You stupid idiot! Look what you've done!" I was insanely ashamed of myself and disgusted. I rushed to the local convenience store to buy rubbing alcohol, which I used to rinse my mouth. I was completely and utterly disgusted with myself and vowed never to have an experience like that ever again.

Of course, that wasn't the last time.

Acting Out of the Closet, Again

On New Year's Eve that year (one day after my twenty-first birthday), my sister and a group of our friends decided to drive up to San Francisco for the extended weekend to celebrate. One of her roommates was from the Bay and let us stay at his parents' house. I was excited to buy alcohol legally for the first time — but not as excited as the under-age friends we'd brought along.

On the night of my birthday, we ended up at a Bubba Gump. When we sat down, I was already shit-faced drunk but decided to order more alcohol, which wasn't the bright-est idea. From what I remember, my sister was sober and not having any of my drunkenness...again. I ended up breaking away from the group and stumbling into a night-club. My sister kept texting and calling me, wondering where I'd disappeared. I told her I was fine and would meet up with them later.

Once I'd sobered up a bit, I somehow made it onto the BART, ready to go home. I called my sister to see where they were, but they'd already left the city and were at our friend's parents' house, wondering when I'd be home. Then I looked up: a set of eyes were fixed directly on me — a man who'd also had too much to drink and was looking for a good time. Curious, I told my sister I was on my way back and would let her know as soon as I got closer.

He got off at a stop and motioned me to follow. We ended up at his hotel. When he entered his room, his friends were already knocked out, and he was hesitant to let me in. I suggested we go to the stairwell. Just like with my first experience, a rush of shame and anxiety filled me thirty seconds into our intimacy. I told him I had to go, and he was confused. I rushed out as he tried to grab me to stay. I avoided his pleading and called my sister to get directions home.

This experience woke me up to my evil and sin, and I contemplated that something needed to change while on our ride home. I also remember projecting my guilt onto my sister during the drive. She shared a vulnerable admission of some of her anxieties. Void of empathy and compassion, I resorted to my way of dealing with complicated situations by compelling her to find Jesus. I was projecting much of my shame onto her, for my words did not match my actions as she witnessed first-hand that dreadful weekend.

New Friends

I had been working at the graphic design firm for over a year, and things were starting to take a turn for the worse. The owner was as shady as shady can be. The office manager had alluded to his misconduct in my initial interview, but I'd decided to overlook it since I was fresh out of a job at the ranch. Moreover, I needed money quickly, so I didn't care what the company was up to; as long as they could pay me, it didn't matter.

Eventually, however, I again had to look for alternative work since the state department had served the owner with a cease-and-desist order. It arrived by certified mail, so someone had to acknowledge receipt. The office manager advised us to ignore it (as she had done over many years,) but it was clear this ship was sinking - fast. I knew I had to get out.

In truth, not everything about the firm was horrible. I met my new best friend Kristina while working there, and she became a trusted confidante: I told her about my struggle with homosexuality. She was Christian, too, but never seemed to judge me for my "backslidden" state. She was quiet at first, but once both of our walls came down, we were best friends. Everyone at work thought we were a couple, which made us laugh — if they only knew! We bonded over this, becoming inseparable.

We talked about my struggle with homosexuality often, as I desired some reprieve. I told Kristina about my fantasies of a straight-marriage family, and she shared hers, too. We imagined being so in love with our spouses that we'd never talk about our pasts ever again. We'd have kids, help see them through their awkward times, and eventually put them through college. But these were our separate visions for ourselves (not with each other). Our conversations continued outside of work, and we started to hang out more.

Eventually, I accepted a new job at a large retail store, while Kristina decided to ride out her career at the shady firm for as long as possible. I was excited by the possibility of meeting new people my age. The store was new to the area, and a lot of college students worked there part-time. I started as a seasonal hire and quickly worked my way into a full-time position. Again, I was excited about this new adventure and quickly became friends with the party crowd.

Defending Jesus

Entering my final year at community college, I sought to return from my embarrassingly eventful and backslidden first two years. I regained confidence in my faith as I became a more vocal advocate when teachers expressed their religious beliefs in class. This wasn't new; I'd sparred with multiple teachers in high school (most notably, my chemistry teacher,) but it became more refined as I acquired new skills in college. I wanted to leave the embarrassing past of my first year and most of my second year behind while I sought a holier life.

I was especially vocal in one of my English classes. The teacher was a hippy of sorts — long grey hair, circular glasses. He smelled of herbs and earth and dressed like a Quaker. He was a staunch agnostic (bordering on atheism) who wasn't afraid to talk about it. He constantly shared about his secular lifestyle with the class, explaining, for example, the meaning behind the rabbit image that surrounded his wedding band (representing his veganism). I couldn't have been more offended by his existence.

This teacher baffled me. He held the complete opposite worldview to my own, and that felt like a threat. He constantly went down rabbit holes (pun intended) about the lack of evidence of the Christian God and openly mocked the Bible. I found every opportunity to refute his feeble claims, bringing out the greatest hits from my high school days. We were constantly at odds, quoting verses and referencing religious materials. It was evident that some students were annoyed by my disruptive personality, telling me to shut the hell up so they could just get their grades and get the hell out of his class.

But I wouldn't back down. I felt it was my duty to convince this man that the Bible was right, regardless of my shame around my past. So I pressed on, thinking I was in a better position than him; at least I acknowledged the one and true God while he worshipped...rabbits, and God only knew what else. My efforts felt futile at first — until two other classmates started taking a similar approach.

New Alliances

Dan and Phil were best friends and roommates and two of the most opposite-looking people you could find. Phil was a sexy surfer, and Dan was an engineering nerd. They tended to be quiet in class until it counted. Once, for example, we were talking about a paper we were required to write. I was doing mine on a subject in Christianity that sought to prove a particular event in the Bible had taken place. The teacher pounced on me like a tiger on its prey (I bet you thought I was going to say rabbit). But the guys came to my rescue, fending off the attack and allowing me to finish my argument.

Sometime after this, Dan and Phil approached me to commend my biblical knowledge and debate skills. They were the friendliest people I'd met in college up to that point. They were kind, fun, and seemed to be genuinely interested in my wellbeing. They wanted to know where I went to church (the Christian version of asking a date, "what do you do for work?"). When they heard I'd been out of a fellowship for quite some time, they told me about their church in a neighboring city named Bayside Church and invited me to join them. I was excited – I'd been looking for a church to redeem my radical ways. They told me I could join them for the Wednesday night service after class. We exchanged information and set the date.

I was ridiculously nervous as I climbed into the back of Phil's truck that Wednesday. I wasn't sure what to expect, but I was desperate for community. I wanted to give this a try even though it was about twenty miles from where I lived.

The service impressed me. The pastor was knowledge-able and persuasive, able to tug on your heartstrings while simultaneously giving you a feast of Biblical knowledge. His style and attentiveness struck me — he seemed to know what his flock needed to hear. Wildly intrigued, I wanted to come back for a Sunday service.

When I shared my experience with Kristina, I was surprised and thrilled to hear that she'd been to this church before and attended every so often. I was pumped — I had a friend to join me at church. It couldn't have been a perfect coincidence, I thought — it was God working his wondrous ways! All signs pointed me in this direction: I had come to Jesus, again.

I also wanted to find a different place to live. My lease with Justin was coming to an end, and there was no way in hell I was going to renew. I knew I was no longer the person I was when I first moved in with him — I was experiencing myself for the first time in college. My wild college antics were coming to an end, and as I felt a renewed sense of responsibility, I asked Dan and Phil if they knew anyone looking for a Christian roommate.

It just so happened that Dan and Phil were moving out of the place they'd been living in with three other guys, and their housemates were looking for their replacements. I was excited about this and interviewed the remaining guys. I decided to move in shortly after meeting them and again felt like I was starting to rebuild my Christian community. My crazy cowboy days were over, and while that community had felt more authentic and genuine, I realized I'd burned too many bridges and needed to get back to my roots.

EXODUS

Shortly after joining Bayside Church, I recommitted my life to Jesus. The insatiable, festering thirst to "have fun" was quenched; I made the hard decision that I was done partying my college days away. I built up the confidence to let my friends know I would try my hand at sobriety. The irony? I gave up drinking at age twenty-one. "Filled with the Spirit," I was a new creation ready to do God's work.

Filled with a renewed sense of meaning and purpose, I chalked up my years of sinfulness to a blip on the radar. I was now back on track, doing God's will. Joining this new church was like joining Jesus' boot camp: it was like nothing I had experienced. The senior pastor was adamant about his convictions and wasn't afraid to let the congregation know about them. He spoke with disdain for sin and was supremely confident that human beings were hopelessly destined to hell unless they converted to Jesus. What could be interpreted as judgmental was portrayed as a concern, as he made passive-aggressive comments about the corrupt state of the secular world.

A constant message preached to believers was that it was paramount that you be a good witness before God — that you had to be an ambassador for the Word of God. Clichéd phrases like, "you may be the only Bible anyone ever reads" became the driving force behind my fear that my dearest friends and family would spend eternity in hell because of my reckless way of life.

One thing heavily pressed upon me in the church was the need to proselytize. I felt it was my duty to be an excellent example to my loved ones by talking about God as much as possible, and I frequently used my 180-degree change in lifestyle as a segue into the topic of God's love. I talked about how my sinful desires had been replaced by God's love — that He alone was now the abundance of my satisfaction. I felt it was my duty to make sure everyone knew about God's transformative love.

Back in the Closet

Equally as intense as my recommitment to Jesus was my homosexual desire. Other than the two incidents already described, I hadn't explored much of my sexuality. I sought a clear biblical definition of what it meant to be a virgin in the Christian context without exposing my deepest, darkest secrets to this new community. I was relieved to find out most people were no longer considered virgins if they had looked on a woman with lust. Evidently, I was in the clear.

I wanted to impress my new church family and be accepted by them, so my homosexuality became a secret between Kristina and me for quite some time. I had a pretty good handle on how to paint an image of myself devoid of any association with homosexuality: make sure not to stare too long at other guys; clear my search history when looking at porn; find ways to share my desire to have a wife and children; be sure to talk about how much of a sin homosexuality was whenever given the opportunity. I could have written the manual on how to be a closeted Christian (stay tuned). But where I looked like I was thriving on the outside, I was struggling on the inside.

Kristina knew the depths of my desperation, as she was the only person I trusted at Bayside Church. I was constantly asked to share my testimony — the personal way God had worked in my life. When it was time for me to share, I outlined my anxiety and depression as a child and how God placed a believer in my life (Amanda from the ice cream shop job) at the most opportune time. "If it hadn't been for her," I pronounced, "I probably wouldn't be standing before you today." I impressed my brothers and sisters in Christ with how well I could tell my dramatic story but kept my deepest secret away from the spotlight.

Eventually, after a Saturday night church service, I came to trust Pastor Ryan, the assistant pastor at the time, with my struggle with homosexuality. The guilt I felt keeping a secret from everyone became overwhelming, and I started by asking him to pray for my family and friends. Eventually, I mustered up the courage to ask him to pray for strength so that I could overcome my struggle with homosexuality. Contrary to my first "coming out" in the church, I didn't pick up on awkwardness from him as he prayed for me to trust the Lord with my feelings and sexuality. I felt free as I became more confident in being the guy who wanted nothing to do with homosexuality and nothing more than to be healed from my affliction.

Walking Through the Wilderness

Shortly after coming out to Ryan, I was introduced to Exodus International through pamphlets in the church information hub. They claimed to be a ministry that helped people who struggled with homosexuality. I was floored by this and curious to learn more.

Exodus seemed to be everything I was looking for. Sure, it was great to have people pray over me to heal me from this affliction. Still, Exodus was an organization that not only understood my struggle first-hand but had a whole ministry dedicated to helping people overcome it. Most fairy tales end with a prince coming to save a princess in distress, but my prince showed up in the form of a conversion therapy organization. I was dreaming big. I couldn't wait to share the news with Kristina.

Kristina did her research, as well, and found that Exodus International held annual conferences with workshops, resources, community, and inspiration to help heal homosexuality. The next conference was in Nashville; we were booked to go to New York the week before, so we decided to go together. We booked our flights, and I kept telling her how excited I was to get some help finally and possibly get healed of my infirmity! It was one thing to have a friend who knew about my affliction; it was a whole other thing to be around a large group of people who understood and shared the same struggle.

We were curious about what people at church would think about Kristina and me going to a conference together and sharing the same hotel room. We weren't yet of the reformed order (the most devout in the church), so we laughed about the possible scandalous church gossip that would circulate should anyone find out. Little did we know this trip would be the last time we'd be able to travel in this "legalism-free" fashion, considering the level of com-

mitment required by our new church and the rules that followed.

On day one of the conference, I walked into the large
room to find Kristina saving a spot for me. It was like walking into a Christian version of a gay club: the large, dark
room was filled with singing and dancing gay men, lifting
their hands in worship while a band played songs of praise.
I was so excited — there were so many fellow Christian homosexuals there! Young, old, men, women - you name it!

When I sat down, I felt a tap on my shoulder. An older
man, looking distressed, asked, "could you please pull up
your pants? It's causing me to stumble." I obliged and apologized, bewildered. Apparently, the crack of my ass was too
much for this man to handle, and this was an excellent example of the fragility of the crowd I soon came to know as
my co-laborers in the fight against homosexuality. Kristina
and I had a good laugh about it afterward. It was a solid introduction to the level of crazy that was about to ensue.

After the band played, the organization's second-in-
command grabbed the mic to make some announcements
and share his testimony about how God had delivered him
from homosexuality. This man struggled with "same-sex
attraction" for many years, partaking in the homosexual
lifestyle and finding no satisfaction. He ultimately committed his life to Jesus and was now pursuing a life of celibacy,
hoping one day to meet his wife and children. We were

dumbfounded and curious. As he made his last emotional, dramatic plea to pursue Jesus for the healing of our sins, he introduced the organization's CEO.

This man was also an interesting fellow. Less flashy than the assistant, he had a similar story — except that he *had* found his wife and had kids. This filled me with hope — here was a man who'd struggled with homosexuality and was now able to lead a normal, heterosexual life. Normal life was being a Christian man attracted to women, marrying, and having kids one day. If this man could find heterosexual love (and he'd been much further in the homosexual life than me before committing his life to Jesus), I thought there was hope for me. I was wildly optimistic after hearing his testimony and excited for the festivities about to commence.

He also expanded on the term used in the assistant's testimony, which had caught my attention: "same-sex attraction." This phrase alone brought new life to me, as it correctly diagnosed my condition: I struggled with "same-sex attraction." This sounded much better than being "gay" or a "homosexual." The phrase "same-sex attraction" assumed that *I* was not the sin I struggled with, but rather that I struggled with an attraction to the same sex. At the time, I didn't consider myself gay or homosexual — I felt these desires were unnatural and not who I was. Same-sex attraction sounded technical — like I had some deformity that could be fixed!

Flirting with Conversion Therapy

After the speeches, we were instructed to select the breakout sessions and workshops we wanted to attend throughout the day. The brochure was filled with workshops, ranging from professionals in conversion therapy to mothers who had famous children who were either active or recovering homosexuals. I was particularly drawn to the leading psychologist of conversion therapy, who was conducting an information workshop on the subject. I circled that along with a few others, and we were off to breakouts.

There were different spaces for different genders and struggles — young men who struggled with same-sex attraction was my group. I was blown away by how many people shared my struggle. Where I felt like an anomaly in my church communities, I no longer felt alone. For the first time, I was in a community where I didn't need to explain my sin to anyone; these men knew exactly how I felt and what I experienced. I finally had a place to call home since I seemed to be the only homosexual in my church (at least, known homosexual). I bonded with a few of the men in attendance, and we exchanged personal information.

There was one man I was drawn to. He had the charisma of a magician, wooing our group with his devilishly wicked ways. His bright smile and caring personality made me weak in the knees. I knew that nothing could come of it -

we were here to get healed! What a waste to spend all that time, money, and energy to end up in bed together. But I knew that my feelings weren't lying to me, so I suppressed them as I had learned early on in life.

We bonded over a story he told about how he was sexually molested as a child by a family member, which evidently resulted in him being gay. Not knowing what that was like, I listened carefully. He continued to tell me about how he had gone off the deep end in college, taking part in homosexual acts. He had a boyfriend at one point but was convicted of his sin. Eventually, he left his homosexual lifestyle to come to this conference and seek healing.

I had no exciting stories to tell him, so I spoke about my family dynamics and how I was convinced that something unknown must have happened to me that turned me gay (nothing ever did, but it was my way of connecting). He told me about how the brain forgets painful memories to protect us. This planted the seed of doubt in questioning my family dynamics, which was later watered in the breakout sessions.

I thought that if this was true about severe traumas, then my brain must have erased the memory to protect me. We friended each other on MySpace, but just like that social media platform, our connection fizzled out after a few phone calls after the conference. I stalked him a bit on social media to see what happened to him. It was evident the information from the conference didn't stick as he was back at his "gay ways." I chalked up our dwindling relationship to God's will.

* * *

After the breakout session, I decided my first workshop would be the one on conversion therapy. There, I met the leader of conversion therapy and got his information, not to mention taking note of his strong personality and handsome face. I ate up his every word, relating to the garbage he was serving up on a "deep personal level."

Some of that garbage included how parental influences could drive homosexuality later in life - i.e., how being gay could result from having a domineering or over-nurturing mother and/or an abusive or distant father. This didn't perfectly describe my family system, but I strained to draw parallels to my own life. I thought about what I learned, how the brain could have erased a painful memory from childhood. My mind pondered more. I wasn't sure if it was the lack of nurturing from my mother or the emotional ineptitude of my father that had resulted in my sinful state. Either way, I trusted this man's expertise and couldn't get enough of his session. I wanted more.

At the end of the workshop, he offered his services. Although he was located in a different state, he could do remote therapy sessions over the phone, and I was interested until I heard about the cost. Due to his exorbitant fees, I decided to find a Christian therapist in my area who practiced conversion therapy.

The other workshops and breakout sessions were just as impactful, and all seemed to point to the successes of conversion therapy. I was enamored by how much I was learning; where I'd begun my grasp of the sin of homosexuality by reading books on the subject, I felt I now had tangible, practical information. I was finally able to see the light at the end of the tunnel; I wasn't alone in my struggle with same-sex attraction. If these other men were able to overcome their sin, I could do the same!

I left the conference on a high, committed to keeping up the momentum by finding a conversion therapy specialist in my area who would accept my medical insurance. I knew that conversion therapy was the answer to healing my homosexuality.

Post-Conference Depression

Coming back to my community was more challenging than I'd imagined. I'd just spent a wonderful week with people who not only understood me but who were going through the same struggle. After leaving the conference bubble, I felt a deep void, sometimes dipping into depression and losing hope of healing. I made sure to get plugged in quickly, out of fear of losing ground in what I'd accomplished at the conference.

After some research, I found a Christian therapist in a neighboring town whose website said he worked with men who struggled with same-sex attraction. He seemed to know the terminology, so I thought I'd give him a chance. I called his office to make sure he wasn't a liberal Christian who believed homosexuality was acceptable. I also wanted to ensure he was skilled in conversion therapy before booking my first appointment. Reassured, I decided to meet with him weekly for as long as it took to overcome my homosexuality.

The therapist turned out to be a white, middle-aged, straight male who was curious about my upbringing. As was the general theme with Evangelicals who believed homosexuality mainly was a condition of upbringing, he inquired about my relationship with my parents. I breezed over my mother since there wasn't much to say. She was a strong-willed individual with whom I cut emotional ties at an early age. My grandmother filled the void in terms of motherly nurturing. He felt that was significant but pressed on about my father.

I shared my desire to gain the acceptance and love of my father. My father was so emotionally closed off, I joked, that sometimes I thought he worked for the FBI or CIA instead of the postal service. He was a man of many secrets yet was my desired source for affirmation. Many sessions examined my childhood to identify the concrete evidence that made me a struggling homosexual man. The process felt numbing until he taught me some techniques to overcome homosexual desires.

He had me imagine a painful or disturbing thought each time I had a homosexual feeling — a very dumbed-down version of shock therapy. He suggested I wear a rubber band around my wrist and flick it whenever I had a homosexual thought. The purpose of this lesson was to associate pain with my homosexuality. I could do these practical things, and I found them more valuable than talking endlessly about my childhood and sexual proclivities. I wanted a quick fix, not a family history lesson or lecture from a straight man who didn't understand where I was coming from.

I eventually became bored by these therapy sessions and made-up excuses not to show up. I decided I needed help discerning what to *do* concerning healing, so I solicited the advice of the senior pastor and assistant pastor Ryan at Bayside Church (whom I'd first told about my sin of homosexuality). I called the church office and made an appointment.

Daddy Issues

Ryan told me about Bayside's discipleship program and said I'd make a fantastic candidate. Discipleship was similar to a mentorship program, where an older, wiser male in the church met with a younger, less mature Christian male to seek guidance and wisdom.

I signed up and was assigned to the husband of a woman I came to call a dear friend. She was enthusiastic, sweet, and kind. On the other hand, her husband was a serious, rural man — a meat-and-potatoes kind of guy. He was also kind but had little experience with young men like me. Although he'd never really dealt with the subject of homosexuality on either a personal or mentorship level, he assured me that our time would be filled with growth and success. He was convinced he'd be able to work with me, so I ended my therapy sessions.

Therapy, in the Christian context of dealing with same-sex attraction, was interesting. On the one hand, homosexuality was (apparently) a product of my sin and rebellion to God; but on the other, it was a byproduct of my upbringing. After reshaping my sad story to one that seemed to fit the narrative of a struggling homosexual (a lesson I learned from conversion therapy), I was told by my disciple (mentor) that it was definitely due to an over-emphasis on nurturing on the part of my mother (that wasn't the case) or related to daddy issues due to a macho-man complex (even further from the truth).

I settled on daddy issues. After all, it was my dad from whom I craved attention and affirmation. But even that didn't seem to fit the narrative of my life; I needed to recreate and exaggerate my past to fit the struggling homosexual narrative.

It was true that my dad was dealt an unfair hand in life - being raised by traditionally Middle Eastern parents in an era that favored secrecy over emotional intimacy. Still, the stories I created about his traumas couldn't have been less true of his reality. I made up stories about my dad, thinking he'd been mistreated as a child – projecting onto his situation beliefs about his upbringing that provided some explanation to my traumas. I knew he had never laid a hand on me; the most hurtful thing he ever did or said to me resulted from a fight between my brother and me — my dad acted out of his nature and lashed out at me for starting the battle.

My dad was a timid, meek man who never laid a hand on or spoke a word against anyone. But his nature and my homosexuality didn't fit the "environmental circumstances" that had apparently created my struggle, so I made up stories to explain my history, attempting to justify why I struggled with same-sex attraction.

As I learned in therapy after leaving the faith, my creation of stories was a way to explain my situation. I needed some reason why my father was the way he was and why I'd ended up the way I had. I learned in actual therapy (since "Christian therapy" was, quite simply, garbage) that it's common for us to make up stories about things we don't know from our past — it helps us understand who we are and why we do what we do. Who I painted my dad to be was the result of me explaining who *I* was in light of my homosexuality, especially since he wasn't open enough to share his own story, and my belief system at the time linked homosexuality to environmental forces.

On My Own, Again

Just like my Christian therapy sessions, sessions with the mentor were short-lived. He eventually told me he felt his work was done — that he couldn't continue with me because I knew so much about the Bible, and he thought he had nothing more to teach me.

It was true — I'd become a fiend for theology. I studied Christianity harder than any subject in class, seeking out seminars, sermons, and books on various Christian subjects. When I wasn't in the church bookstore, you could find me at the local Christian bookstore, scanning the shelves for new material. I spent more money than God learning about ... Him. I could quote the Bible even better than my mentor, which left me to my own devices.

I also learned more about same-sex attraction. I constantly checked the Exodus International website for resources and recommendations. The Christian bookstore had a sex education section that became my go-to. I became a master at skimming articles to see which way they leaned — in favor of homosexuality in the church or not. If it was more liberal, I disregarded it and prayed for the writer - that their eyes would be opened to the truth.

In church, I learned that theologians who believed in such deviant beliefs were considered false teachers and would be relegated to a special place in hell. This became a helpful tool — disregarding someone's interpretation of the scriptures if they didn't align with my ultra-conservative theological beliefs; I simply believed they were false teachers and could ignore their perspective.

Militant Behavior

I couldn't get enough literature about same-sex attraction. My disdain for homosexuality soared to new heights when I came across *Marriage Under Fire,* a book by a locko-loony bin of a man named James Dobson. In it, I learned there was a war going on for the souls of my family and friends. I learned that my homosexuality was an assault on

God, that it was an abomination. It was my duty as a believer to rebuke homosexuality at all costs and defend traditional marriage. If God were to bless me with a wife, I'd have to first hold up my end of the deal by castigating my homosexual tendencies.

I hated myself even more.

This coincided with California voting on an amendment to the state's constitution that would ban same-sex marriage, known as Proposition 8. Along with many in the area, my church was up in arms over the idea of same-sex marriage — it was, we believed, the gateway to pedophilia and beastiality. It was an absolute abomination to allow two people of the same sex who loved each other to enter holy matrimony, for it was ultimately God who oversaw marriage. God "clearly" defined marriage as a relationship between one man and one woman (unless you were of the Old Testament, in which case, what the hell, men could marry as many women as they wanted!).

The association of homosexuality with pedophilia and beastiality alone was enough to make me despise the thought of gay marriage. Over my dead body would I allow this sinister sin to define me.

THOUGHT: BELONGING

Recently, my brother and I watched a cooking competition show together and analyzed why a particular character was so annoying. He constantly spoke about how he was doing *this* for his husband, cooking *that* for his husband, and wanting to be a better *cook*. We found him off-putting; why did he constantly have to talk about his husband? It felt like he was overcompensating for something.

Then it dawned on me: this was a form of internalized homophobia. Had it been a heterosexual man talking about his wife, it would've gone unnoticed or possibly come off as endearing. But because this man was talking about his homosexual relationship, it felt unnatural and over the top. Both my brother and I now live our true natures as homosexual men, but it still bothered us. It occurred to me that our conditioning of heterosexual norms still had it feel unnatural to watch one of our own being his free self on national television.

I believe there's more homophobia in the gay community than in any other. For many homosexuals, our upbringing was influenced by belief systems that told us that the essence of who we were was wrong and repulsive. Whether raised in a religious or secular home, the Judeo-Christian belief system is predominant in American culture. Its principles in our school system include the "Golden Rule," which is modeled after biblical teachings. We're taught that our country was founded on Judeo-Christian beliefs, which are subconsciously embedded in our culture and shape our worldview (not to mention that popular culture and advertisement catered almost exclusively to hetero norms until recently).

In this belief system, those who are homosexual grow up believing something is wrong with them, which sets them on a helpless path. In never really belonging to ourselves, we seek to belong to others. We compromise aspects of us we think will be unappealing to others, not realizing that those traits are most beautiful, for they are the essence of who we are.

On the quest to be accepted by anyone who'll take a chance on us, we deny aspects of ourselves that we were led to believe were wrong or repulsive. When we're taught something like that at such an early age, we hardwire specific neural pathways — pathways that turn us against ourselves. The greatest challenge of our lives, then, is to undo the programming and conditioning of our youth to learn how to love and accept ourselves as we are.

Not a Sinner

As a former self-hating Christian, one of the most complex struggles I had to make it through was to accept that I wasn't a dirty, rotten sinner.

The primary source of my identity as such was rooted in my homosexuality. Undoing the belief that "I'm unworthy of anything good because of who I am" is something I work on to this day. I must constantly catch myself when I'm self-hating, bringing to consciousness the hate-filled thought and denouncing it.

This mentality is so pervasive that it struck at the very core of my identity as a man. For example, in the lead-up to one of my therapy sessions, I wrestled with the thought: am I a narcissist? It seemed I constantly thought about myself — how stupid, inefficient, undesirable, or unattractive I was. When I brought this up in therapy, Dr. Rachael's response couldn't have been more surprising: "You aren't a narcissist, and your wonder about whether you are is proof of it. Narcissists don't worry about being narcissists. For as long as I've known you, the theme has always been that all you've ever wanted in life was to belong."

Belong. That's it! That's all I've ever wanted in life. It dawned on me that that was why I joined the church in the first place — to feel like I belonged to something. I wanted to belong to my dad and pursued Republican politics as a way of connecting and gaining acceptance. Then I joined the Christian faith to belong to a group that promised to deliver me from the one thing I believed would have cast me out of belonging to my family. The church provided clear guidelines to belong to them, and I was more than happy to oblige...out of fear of losing my community.

Community. It was the single thread holding me together. I knew in my heart of hearts that my belief system was a crock of bullshit. How could a thousands-year-old book be the absolute truth for all humanity? The fear of losing my community was the most potent force keeping me devoted to the faith.

After watching a documentary with a friend on the Flat Earther movement, I was enlightened. Forty-five minutes into the documentary, we laughed about the insane shit these people believed. But the most enlightening scene filled the mind of my own reckless devotion.

The moderator of an astronomy group opened by questioning the belief system of the Flat Earthers. The audience laughed in amusement until the moderator mentioned how these people were devoted not out of conviction but fear. Fear of losing their community. Fear of being ostracized. Fear of being humiliated by assimilating to "secular culture." The fear of losing their community was more potent than the fear of facing the truth of their doubt. It only pushed them deeper into their belief system when faced with hard facts, for it was their only chance to form some sort of community. Had they renounced their faith, they would be ostracized by the Flat Earther community and humiliated before secular society. Reintegrating into secular society would become one of the most dreadful experiences, so trusting in their compromised belief system was their only choice. That night, I became enlightened to my struggle and subsequent departure.

I was afraid of losing the only people who "got me." I was scared to face the people I had condemned to hell for their lack of faith in "absolute truth." But at some point, the fear of losing myself became more potent than the loss of my community. Ultimately, I chose to be genuine to myself than become recklessly devoted to those who were living a lie.

Belonging was why I pressed on in the faith even though huge doubts welled up within me. The fear of losing my community was more powerful than the urge to leave. The fear of not belonging to something or someone was overwhelming. A sense of belonging was the only thing keeping me together, and I was afraid that if I let it go, I'd spiral out of connection and control. I would have lost my identity; the essence of who I was belonged to my faith.

When I finally did leave the church, I had night terrors - a direct result of no longer belonging to a community. I was forced to find a new community, which was one of the hardest things I'd ever had to do. I repeatedly contemplated going back to a church in the area just because I was lonely. In fact, shortly after moving to Los Angeles, I did start attending a megachurch downtown, but it didn't feel right. I was no longer a believer, and the rules of Evangelical Christianity no longer applied to me. I knew my authentic sexuality was a complete contradiction to their teachings.

At that moment, it occurred to me that the power of "not belonging" didn't hold the same weight as it had in times past. I was growing. I was learning who I was and what I wanted to build in my life. I could choose to form a new community that accepted me for who I am, not who I could "become" to be taken in.

It wasn't until (secular) therapy that I was able to realize that the process of belonging to myself had started sooner than I'd imagined. What I wanted more than anything in life was to belong, and it all had to begin with belonging to myself. For a long time, I compromised who I was to belong to others, but I was learning how to accept myself for the first time. I started saying no to things that no longer served me and embraced things that did. I needed to belong first to the one person I'd been running from for so long: myself.

PART

3

OH, HOLY ROLLIN' DAYS

NEW BEGINNINGS

Now back to college. Over time, I committed my life fully to Bayside Church. I couldn't get enough of it. It started slowly at first; I only went to Sunday services. Eventually, though, I was at church four times a week: Wednesday night service, men's Bible study, Saturday night service, and serving during Sunday service.

I decided to join the ushering team on Sunday mornings because it was an excellent way to meet new people. I was assigned to greet the congregation on Sundays as they trickled in — handing out church bulletins with a warm welcome. Once service started, it was my job to sit in the back row and wait to help with the offering of communion, meaning passing around a plate filled with individual cups of grape juice and broken crackers.

I was beginning a new path of service to my faith, and it felt amazing. Being at church gave me a renewed sense of purpose as I formed bonds with a new community. I was eager to learn the language of this church; I made sure to address the pastors with formalities and sprinkle in "Praise the Lords" as often as possible. As I volunteered more, I got noticed by congregants. They saw a familiar face and desired to know more. Ultimately, I wanted to dive in deeper, so I decided to join a weekday night bible study.

Bible Study

Bible study is where Christians go during the week to go over a particular book of the Bible or dive deeper into a subject to expand knowledge of the faith. It was how the most devout kept each other accountable — talking about different events in our lives and praying for loved ones we wanted to come to know Jesus.

In reality, it was a place to gossip; you talked about the drama and people in your lives while clothing it in a prayer request. Unlike Real Life Church, Bayside only had gender-specific groups, meaning men and women were not allowed to be in the same Bible study group unless they were in the group for married couples. My only option was the single men's Bible study. In hindsight, it would've been less of a temptation for me to be in the women's Bible study.

Bible study was where I got to shine. The group was full of men of different ages and backgrounds. Some, like me, were new to the church, while others had been committed members for years. The best part was that church leaders led the group. To get a feel for the group, I decided to stay silent for my first few visits — I'd be a bystander assessing the trustworthiness of the men in the group. I knew I couldn't just lay all my cards out right away; I had too much to lose if they found out about my struggle with same-sex attraction before getting to know me.

Being a struggling homosexual wasn't the best look at Bayside, regardless of your devotion or quest to seek deliverance from it. Before exposing my deepest secrets to a group of men I feared wouldn't understand the struggle, I needed time. My experience supported my reservations, as the ignorance of those who didn't understand same-sex attraction rose to the surface; some men perceived homosexuals as having a sexual appetite for all men. By the stringent rules of this church body, I also assumed these were the types of Christians who associated homosexuality with pedophilia and beastiality. Exposing myself was not a risk I was willing to take.

My suspicions were not paranoid, and my fear of being misunderstood was borne out. When I eventually came out to the group, I was met with curiosity and caution. I could read the room, and the body language suggested that for some, it was like all the air had just been sucked out. Others were uncomfortable just being so close to a homosexual. For others, it was like a switch turned — they began talking to me differently, watching every word they spoke around me. It was how I imagined a black person might feel when approached by racist white people trying to be careful about which words they used and how they conducted themselves. I was now the token homosexual of the group.

I remember some men admitting that they didn't want to become a "stumbling block" to me - a church term for someone or something that tempts someone in their specific weakness — i.e., a sexy, shirtless man for someone struggling with same-sex attraction. Or, in this context, a straight man who was *way* too confident about his looks. I had to reassure them that they had nothing to worry about - they were in no way a stumbling block to me. I internally rolled my eyes and laughed about it later.

My admittance often led to a different conversation, as I had to explain that my attraction to men was no different than their attraction to women — I wasn't attracted to all men just as they weren't attracted to all women. What I wanted to say was, "I'm not attracted to everyone with a penis, just as I hope you aren't to everyone with a vagina." It was like teaching kindergarteners, but the best part was that I could control the narrative. Sometimes I couldn't wait to share a story with Kristina, wondering what the hell was wrong with people. I sometimes clothed my explanations in prayer requests for specific people who asked if shit really got crazy.

Submitting to Leadership

My efforts in Bible study didn't go unnoticed. I brought a depth of knowledge and vulnerability that had been lacking before I joined. Having been self-taught since high school, I leveraged resources from my past to the topic at hand. For instance, when we discussed a Bible verse describing the greatness of God's creation, my thoughts on the cosmos based on a documentary by a famous Christian "astronomer" came in handy.

I was a rising star in the group; my ability to quote scriptures and carry on meaningful conversations caused others to think deeply about their faith. Members of the church leadership team in this Bible study group were intrigued by my curiosity and knowledge. Gordon, the pastor who oversaw Bible study, became curious about my abilities. He was the pastor of the Bible college and a very peculiar man (more on him in an upcoming chapter).

I wasn't often exposed to church leadership. During Wednesday, Saturday, and Sunday services, most leaders were busy doing their jobs, attending to other congregants. Bible study was a much more intimate setting and allowed me to show my true colors. Not long after joining the group, I was asked to take on more responsibilities at the church.

Looking back, I see that what was attractive to leadership was less my fundamental knowledge than my willingness to submit to authority figures. At a very early age, I learned that the best way to become accepted by some people is to honor and respect their title. I then realized that there are no more fragile egos in the world than those of Evangelical pastors. Stroking their egos was the way to their hearts.

A hallmark of my style of submission was using lots of formalities and being obsequious. Thus, even though it was preached that everyone was equal in the eyes of God, there were those who God seemed to speak with more favor – hence the creation of the Evangelical pastor.

The structure of Bayside Church resembled more of a ranking scale. Most Evangelical churches are structured like the executive branch of the government, where there's a president and their cabinet. The church leader oversees the church's general operations (the "president") and delegates duties to junior pastors (the "cabinet").

At Bayside, the senior pastor oversaw and taught the entire church - think president. He made final decisions, along with the board of advisors, for significant decisions, like church-building projects and substantial monetary allocations. The assistant pastor was second-in-command and heir to the church if the senior pastor were to leave - think vice president. The assistant pastor was responsible for announcements and anything relegated to him by the senior pastor (the church bitch). Then there were junior pastors, who fell into the categories of missionary work (international proselytizing,) youth, and a few other titles sprinkled among the different ministries that made up this church - the cabinet.

I learned early on that there was a clear hierarchy, which was strictly enforced and revered. The air was thick with patriarchy and loyalty, as it was evident that the alpha male was the true leader. I admired many leaders, thinking they were better than me because they knew more about God. After all, they had to communicate directly with Him to lead the church. The pecking order also reinforced my strong sense of obligation to follow the rules and be respectful. I thought I was honoring God's ordained structure, which would facilitate "advancement of the gospel" — a concept often preached to highlight the need to honor and submit to church leadership.

But what was really going in me was more deceitful than respecting the leaders: it was fear.

Fear & Trembling

The fear of losing my Bayside community was one of the most powerful forces that kept me obedient. I constantly found myself submitting to what was, I felt at times, irrational rules. Unfortunately, these rules were commonly accepted by the most devout of the church, and to be in the "in-group," I needed to relinquish certain rights. This was a matter of survival, as my church family became even more important than my blood family.

As I started to get more involved in the church, I formed alliances with many people. It felt amazing to have such an extensive network of like-minded individuals all striving to accomplish the essential thing in life: grow in the love of Jesus and share His message of salvation. We constantly prayed with each other, recognizing the "lost souls" in our lives that we wanted to see come to Jesus. This unified message — that there were people in our lives who needed saving — only solidified the bond between us, as we each experienced some sort of distancing from family members and friends.

This sense of separation often became a self-fulfilling prophecy, as more and more people in my life outside of the church began distancing themselves from me due to my radical and judgmental views. With only my church family to accept, support, and understand me, I clung even harder to the faith, praying fervently that my loved ones would one day come to know the "one and only savior, Jesus Christ."

It was common for the most devout in the faith to experience forms of what we called "persecution" — to the point of being completely ostracized from family gatherings because we chose to follow Jesus. Those who experienced such condemnation were forced to choose between family or faith, but as we became more devoted to the church, making that choice wasn't hard at all.

Knowing what I know now, it's baffling that such a message would cause fervent devotion. And if it had happened all at once, it would've been painfully obvious. But the church's tactic was to strip away common sense slowly and incrementally. I was especially terrified about the doctrine of eternal damnation being what awaited my family and loved ones if they weren't saved; this instilled enough fear in me to press on. Most churches were less militant about their beliefs and approach, but this Evangelical church took the message of salvation very seriously.

At the time, I wholeheartedly believed in this dark prophetic fate: that my loved ones who didn't know Jesus would be damned to hell. And while the church said salvation was an individual choice, it was implied that the burden of the salvation of the unsaved fell on the shoulders of the believers in their life (namely, me). This was more intense than the teachings at the church of my youth — I now felt it was my responsibility to be the perfect representation of faith to the lost souls in my life, both in action and in word. I constantly feared that if I weren't an excellent example of Jesus (by, among other things, preaching the salvation message), a large part of their eternal damnation would be my fault.

One way to be a good witness of Jesus was to spend time reading the Bible and being sensitive to particular convictions "revealed to us by the Holy Spirit." These times were called our "devotionals" and were usually conducted when you were alone, first thing in the morning or at night before bed. Adopting such practices by choosing to be in "the Word" rather than partaking in sinful acts became safeguards against sin.

Our actions were also judged. After time in devotional, we were told to wait for the Spirit to guide us on what convictions could prevent us from partaking in certain acts. This could be, for example, staying away from people or places that triggered the desire to sin. For me, this meant avoiding parties, bars, and clubs because it was easy for me to get drunk and "blow my witness" to others around me since we were called to be witnesses of Jesus' salvation to the "sinful world." "Blowing your witness" would make the outside world question your faith if you partook in sinful acts. Thus, becoming "less like the world" and becoming "more like Jesus" was our highest calling as a Christian.

This propagated the lifestyle of isolation and co-dependency on our church family.

Upping the Ante

At Bayside, we were constantly taught that for our loved ones to come to know Jesus, we not only had to be good examples of Christ but (relentlessly) share the good news of salvation. Therefore, if I were to be a faithful follower, I needed to look like Jesus *and* share about Jesus. Since I had some experience preaching the gospel in high school, I thought this would be a piece of cake.

What was different about this church was its approach: aside from being adamant about the need to stay away from the image of sin by remaining obedient to our convictions, they leveraged the power of evangelism — the art of proselytizing. I thought I'd learned everything I needed to know about evangelism, but I soon discovered I'd merely scratched the surface. For this church, proselytizing was a masterpiece; they doubled down on "working out your salvation with fear and trembling."

We were constantly taught tactics for approaching non-believers. One was learning how to tell your testimony. We were instructed to prepare a 30-second, 2-minute, and 30-minute story about how Jesus had saved our lives and how He was willing to do the same for the unbeliever. *"You could never refute a testimony because it is your story. Nobody can refute your story."* We needed to be ready to share the gospel of Jesus Christ at any moment, with anyone, and always advised to have something prepared to say.

The gospel was the only thing that brought us back into communion with God, so it became my burden to make sure my loved ones knew of their imminent fate should they refuse the "gospel of Jesus." The heaviest on my heart were my immediate family members: my dad, mom, brother, and sister. I believed it was my duty to show them the love of Jesus, that they would see how I had changed and want the same transformation for their lives by my example. We believed the gospel of Jesus was a doctrine of absolute truth, and I needed to save my family.

My tenacity in "preaching the gospel" became a source of inspiration to many in the church, especially those in leadership. I constantly prayed for my family members and loved ones, asking that my brothers and sisters in Christ would join me in praying that the "Holy Spirit would guide my blood brother and sister to Jesus" (another strange doctrinal belief). I was repeatedly praised for how zealous I was in getting the good news of Jesus out there. I volunteered for outreach ministry opportunities and took multiple classes on how to evangelize. I was crazy for it and wanted everyone in my life to know Jesus. But my utmost desire was reserved for one specific person in my life: my dad.

Saving Dad

One of my proudest moments was leading my dad to Jesus. Over a few months, I visited home a few times for special occasions, like birthdays and holidays. My relationship with my dad weighed heavy on my heart as I tried to find some way to connect with him.

Outside occasionally protesting alongside pro-lifers at the local Planned Parenthood or engaging in pro-Israel propaganda, I was no longer interested in politics. This meant my father and I had lost our common bond. Where politics had once united us, a gap of silence now lay between us. We talked extensively about the weather and little about life, and the space between us ate at me. I wondered if the same-sex attraction experts were right: Perhaps issues in my relationship with my dad were the cause of my homosexuality.

I constantly prayed with my roommates and fellow Bible study members to find some way to share the gospel with my dad. Finally, after much deliberation, prayer, and contemplation, I decided to share a part of my testimony with my father. After practicing with some people from church,

I had it down pat. I just needed the right moment to approach him about Jesus.

We were walking around the local mall when I decided to go for it. I told him I had something to share and began telling him how I'd struggled with same-sex attraction. Suddenly, I noticed he was a few steps ahead of me — his stride had dramatically lengthened. I tried to catch up with him, but he wouldn't even acknowledge me. I was scared by his reaction, for I knew he had the wrong interpretation — he hadn't let me finish my story.

We got in the car and headed home, my sister in the back seat. I tried to clear things up — to let him know why I'd brought this whole thing up in the first place. He kept avoiding me until we walked up to the door, and I cornered him. I told him to hear me out — that Jesus was healing me from same-sex attraction and that the same salvation Jesus had given to me, He could do for my dad.

My father finally lifted his head to look at me as he started to quiver. It sent chills down my spine to see him like this; for the first time, I was looking into the soul of my dad, seeing his vulnerability as he hesitantly replied to my plea for a response. I saw something more genuine than the message I was pressing upon him but continued in my discomfort. I didn't know what to say; all I knew was that my dad needed Jesus more than anyone I could imagine.

The next time I visited, I refrained from sharing my testimony, knowing it would shut him down. I knew he couldn't handle another son being gay, even though I was in the process of being healed from it. He was a product of his generation, and I knew he would internalize responsibility for having two gay sons. His culture had taught him that homosexuality was a byproduct of childrearing; that the result of a gay child was the burden of the parents. So, I stuck to the subject at hand: his salvation.

He was interested in what I had to say, so I kept telling him more. I quoted verses from the book of Romans, my favorite book in the Bible at the time for its clear judgment of sin and explanation of salvation. This started a whole new avenue of dialogue with my dad. He was intrigued by this form of salvation. When I asked if he wanted to accept Jesus into his life, he said yes. I led him into the prayer, and he received. No longer were the topics between us surface-level, as he decided to let Jesus into his heart and life...on my watch.

As much as the church had become my chosen family, I still desperately desired the approval and acceptance of my dad. So, when he eventually "gave his life to Jesus" after I prayed the "sinner's prayer" with him (the prayer someone prays when they want to become a Christian), I was overjoyed. I couldn't believe my dad had accepted Jesus; a whole new way of connecting with him was beginning. Of course, this also bought me brownie points and bragging rights at the subsequent Bible study, as we prayed in thanks to God for the victory of me winning over my dad.

The Convictions of Others

Over time, I was asked to take on further responsibilities within Bayside Church. With greater responsibility came more tremendous sacrifice, which I was more than willing to accept. Finally, I was living the dream — I'd gained the respect of leadership and was deemed worthy enough to serve in greater capacities. Little did I know that the steady trickle of compromising my freedoms and convictions would be the beginning of a more complex form of control and manipulation.

Anyone who took on greater leadership responsibilities within this church was required to follow a specific set of rules. This was a way of ensuring submission to those who held power. The most basic rules were certain "convictions" of the senior pastor, which leaders had to adopt with the intent to be a "good witness" to the other congregants. This was like a form of initiation — proof that you were worthy enough to serve God. If you were obedient to the pastor's convictions, you were moldable to their image of what it meant to be a leader. Examples of poor leadership in the Bible were used as examples of what could happen if you

| 186 |

gave into temptations, so the rules were a safeguard to keep us accountable.

I chose to volunteer with the youth group, so I met with the youth pastor and Ryan. We went over the rules that applied to all leaders in the church and specific regulations concerning the youth group. The senior pastor had a conviction about alcohol (his personal experiences drove him to despise the stuff). He impressed upon all leaders at Bayside the need to abstain from consuming any form of alcohol at any time, whether in public or private. As a result, I could no longer be associated with alcohol in any way for fear of someone seeing me "stumble." This went beyond my personal conviction of avoiding bars and clubs, as I was now not even to be in a place that had alcohol at all or have it in the privacy of my home.

In addition, the observations of others in the church caused me to be required to follow another, different kind of rule: Apparently, it didn't look good to leadership that I was strangely close to women without having some sort of romantic relationship with them. It was frowned upon for men to be "just friends" with females — the logic being that ultimately those types of friendships resulted in lust since this was the sinful nature of relationships between men and women.

Kristina and I were best friends, and it seemed like we were a "love couple" to some in the church. However, we were inseparable, especially as we were both in a newer environment, and she was my biggest confidant when it came to my sin of homosexuality. Kristina and I were no exception to the rules, though, and I was asked to adopt the mandate that men maintain a safe distance from women; there was no exception for a struggling homosexual because of the precedent it would set.

Men were expected to have another person present when hanging out with women (unless you were a couple) and to keep a door open if in a room alone. It was frowned upon for women to spend time with men late at night, for that's when the "desire of lust" was most present. Women were also required to dress modestly as not to cause men in the church to stumble. It finally made sense to me why there were no co-ed Bible studies at the church.

You'd have thought they'd gotten these rules from *1984* (a book I've picked up and put down many times since it triggers memories of this control), and the influence of the senior pastor was evident in his teaching style. He was well-known for sermons that passively-aggressively implored congregants to take up his convictions. He supposedly left it up to the Holy Spirit to convict those who didn't see it his way but made it non-negotiable for those in leadership to adopt his convictions. The rules got even stricter as I climbed the leadership ladder, but these were sacrifices I was willing to make.

Willing to Sacrifice

Committing fully to my church wasn't hard for me — I thoroughly enjoyed the attention I received as a result. Doing more meant I was noticed more by leadership, which gave me a sense of home as I belonged. This was a feeling I later came to realize had been missing for quite some time. My imprint was small at first, but as I joined in activities that seemed of interest only to the most devout, I made a name for myself. Slowly but surely, my impact was noticed, and it felt amazing.

My whole Christian life was a quest to find belonging. That was made apparent to me later, in therapy, during my actual "coming out" phase. I was forever looking for ways to belong to someone and something. The church killed two birds with one stone in this respect: it provided a sense of community and (supposedly) healed the parts I found most repulsive. It was a no-brainer at the time: if I had a group that accepted me, I'd do *anything* to hold onto that – even if that acceptance came with severe conditions.

I constantly felt like a wanderer, a vagabond; I relentlessly sought a place of belonging. When I thought I'd finally found a place to rest, following the rules was nothing but a means to stay connected to the community. If this meant, at first, giving up alcohol and female friends, I was more than willing to make the sacrifice.

Bible College

As I neared the end of obtaining my third associate degree at my community college, it was time to make a cru-
cial decision about my studies. I'd moved to the area for
several reasons, one of which was to eventually transfer to
the local four-year college, which was well-known for its
accounting program. The community college had a high
transfer rate to this prestigious college, primarily because
half of the community college teachers worked at the four-
year college, too. I thought it would be wise to maintain
an excellent academic profile at the community college to
increase my chances of getting into a bachelor's program.
Gaining a degree from this university would, I believed, set
me on a path to success in the professional world.

One of my most significant influences in community
college was a quirky attorney who taught business law. I
was introduced to her in my earlier years, and she fascinated me – she spoke passionately about the legal system
and how the government worked. Enamored by her passion
and tenacity, I attended her office hours more frequently
than your average undergraduate. Essentially, I became the
teacher's pet through my constant inquiry and responsive-
ness in class.

She took note and inquired about my career interests. I
was frank with her: I'd never considered a law degree until

she'd brought it up. However, I was fascinated by the world of legal studies, how it involved interpreting the law and making it applicable to the case you were arguing. With her guidance, I sought out opportunities for real-world experience.

I came across a Craigslist ad for an intern-to-full-time position at a law firm. When I applied, little did I know that this firm was one of the most successful and notorious in the county, made famous by a case about a local college girl who'd gone missing years before I'd moved to the area.

After my interview, I won the affection of the office manager, who it turned out was married to the founding partner. I was invited to interview with the partner the same day, and after pledging my utmost loyalty to the firm, I was offered the position on the spot. Hand-selected out of 200 applicants, I knew the stakes were high.

The founding partner took me under his wing. He was a strange person, and I desired to gain his approval. I was assigned to be his direct assistant and promised a full scholarship to law school if I proved loyal. However, my interest in his peculiar personality took a turn for the worse after attending a lunch with him and his staff.

Shortly after being seated, the partner asked the waiter for crayons. The tablecloth was butcher paper, and he started doodling on it, drawing a picture of the globe with a stick figurine on top of it, with money-sign sunglasses on. He said it was a "self-portrait." It made me uncomfortable to see an adult so respected and highly regarded in his industry resort to such childish antics.

After this awkward lunch, he showed me around town in his brand-new Escalade. This turned out to be an exercise in self-indulgence — he pointed out his many properties, everything from rural farmhouses to extravagant mansions. At the end of the trip, he told me that one day, this could be me. I could have all the possessions I ever wanted if I were a hard worker. My lack of enthusiasm was due in part to my aspirations to impress church leadership.

Alternatively, shortly after joining Bayside Church, I realized that I could get my bachelor's degree in biblical studies at their satellite Bible college campus. During my time at the law firm, I was auditing my first Bible college course and constantly seeking leadership advice about which path to choose: the professional career path or the "godly" path of becoming a pastor. I listened to the testimony of church leaders who'd decided to give up careers in engineering and the like to work full-time in the church. Between the discomfort I felt at the law firm and hearing stories of those who'd sacrificed it all for the sake of "the gospel" (by attending Bible college), I thought this was a test — that the Lord was testing my loyalty.

One night in Bible class, I made a hasty decision. After only two weeks at the law firm, I called the office manager to let her know I was no longer interested in the position because I was pursuing a career as a pastor. That night, I also quit applying to the four-year university for an accounting degree, even though my experience in "the world" had nothing to do with accounting (accounting was a career I had thought about sometime in high school. My dad was an accounting major and considering my desires to please him, you can probably piece together the puzzle from here). Instead, I enrolled full-time in Bible college. I called my dad to let him know the news, to which he hesitantly said, "If this is what you want." I felt like I'd made the right decision and let my dad know this *was* what I wanted. I also thought this would earn me brownie points with the church leadership.

My decision to attend Bible college wasn't just about learning more about the Bible and eventually becoming a pastor. I also loved the attention I was getting at church, as leaders took more significant notice of my actions and loyalty to the faith. It felt amazing to have people's attention at the top, and I felt like I mattered. I didn't think accounting or law would bring me the same kind of satisfaction.

The One In Need of Saving

Bible college empowered me with knowledge, emboldening my madness. Sure, I was drinking the Kool-Aid long before Bible college, but this gave me extra conviction. I became determined to convert every person in my life, sometimes even finding time to talk to the drive-through clerk at McDonald's. I became a "vessel" — I started a blog called "A Vessel for His Glory" (since deleted). Little did I know what a tool I had become.

My determination to convert others only generated an even more significant gap between my siblings and me. When my family or friends pushed back on my proselytizing, I considered it prophetic. I constantly referred to the Bible verse that talks about how Jesus came to divide families, friends, etc. My Bible knowledge became one of the greatest weapons in my arsenal, and I could quote scriptures like never before and often did.

Bible college gave me more Bible verses and story references to draw from. When met with reason and common sense, I simply interpreted from scriptures that the world was blind to God's truth and that the world's wisdom was foolishness. I also gleaned stories of prophets in the Old Testament from my studies, learning how some were persecuted for their belief in God and started invoking them as if they paralleled my own experience. Nothing held me

MY GAY CHURCH DAYS

back except the intense loneliness I felt, which continued to push me further into fellowship with those who thought like me.

I later learned that this kind of loneliness is a common form of psychological manipulation used by cults and extreme belief systems to keep people dependent. My fear of alone became the single most powerful tool to keep me in submission to the control of this church. Moments of doubt in my faith only pushed me further into submission, as the fear of losing my community made me more persistent in preaching the gospel of Jesus.

My sister once saw the pendulum swing to one side; she now witnessed the swing to the other. Where she had once saved me, I now felt the need to save her. She became a constant recipient of my proselytizing; I found any and every opportunity to share with her my newfound life. I longed for her to find the same "joy" I found and preached the gospel to her in her most vulnerable moments. But, instead, she was stronger than I ever imagined as she sat silently, patiently waiting for me to finish getting off my soapbox. She knew who I was and who I was pretending to be, but she persisted in her love for me and never left my side.

In retrospect, she was the only constant in my life. She never hung me out to dry, regardless of how batshit crazy things got. Where she'd once picked my drunk ass up off the concrete to help me avoid getting a public disorderly conduct violation, we now couldn't even have a simple dinner without me going on about how Jesus had saved me and how He could do the same for her. Her love was consistent, and so was her truth.

It became clear to me after leaving the faith that I was the one that genuinely needed saving.

Ulterior Motives

What also drew me to Bible college was that Jake, my housemate, was enrolled in it full-time. His parents, devout Christians themselves, were devoting their resources to seeing him pursue the ministry. Jake was a gifted musician and charismatic leader; everyone felt small in his presence. He was kind, loving, caring, and compassionate. It's what drew me to him the most — his love for people and the Lord.

One night, Jake shared a passage with me about what it meant to be a man. His father had shared it with him, obviously meaning for it to be reassuring. The quote stated that to the Lord, manliness was more than just being a strong, strapping alpha male. It meant being a "man after the Lord's heart" — a phrase so common in the church it could have been found in the home décor section of a Ross.

This specific passage not only made sense to me but had me realize that Jake, too, struggled with what it meant to be a man. His father had once imparted a verse to remind him what true manliness looked like to the one who mattered most: God. Jake wasn't your stereotypical alpha male. He was charming, handsome, and charismatic. He could swoon the pants off anyone, especially the single women at church. Everyone was in love with Jake, while some questioned his sexuality. However, that didn't stop him from being himself, which to my sudden surprise, became similar to me.

JAKE

This is a story even Taylor Swift couldn't write. You know: Prince Charming is perfect in every way and presents himself to the helpless damsel in distress.

Between joining the church and attending Bible college, I felt like I was outgrowing my roommate situation. The more I leaned into leadership, the more I compared myself to other Christians, assessing the worthiness of their faith. I thought of myself as a better Christian than my "supposed" Christian roommates because I was more devoted through service and proselytizing. Comparing myself to others was my spice of life, learned mainly from Bayside's senior pastor and leaders.

Church leaders constantly talked about how our church was better than others, more devoted to the faith, and furthering the gospel of Jesus more than other churches in the area. At first, I had no qualms about their judgment and comparison. After all, they were speaking my language - wildly insecure, I constantly compared myself to others to make myself feel better.

I found my housemates off-putting and questioned their faith, often praying with my fellow congregants for a better, "more Godly" living situation (yet another example of how the catty judgment of others clothed in prayer was a staple of this church). One of my housemates couldn't keep his door closed while watching porn, while another spent 45 minutes "showering" every day (another housemate and I jokingly wondered if there was any skin left after the constant stroking). I was friends with the other two housemates, but it was clear the environment wasn't the best for my growth as a Christian; I desired something more accountable.

Although my homosexuality was kept in check in public, I found ways to get around accountability software and cleared my search history when viewing gay porn on community Wi-Fi. At home, I learned to turn off my cell phone's Wi-Fi connection or download porn videos to my computer not to be detected by my housemates. I also mastered the art of looking at porn in public without being detected (i.e., a place in the library where no one could see my screen). Where my public appearance of suppression seemed to be going well, secrecy became the lifeblood of release.

During my last semester at community college (and shortly after choosing Bible college over pursuing a four-year degree), I became acquainted with what was known as "the guys' house." A group of five guys lived together in a condo three blocks away from the church. They were all known for their devotion to the faith. This was also where Phil and Dan lived, and since Phil was looking to move on, a spot in the guys' house was opening up.

After class, I was invited to go over to their house to be interviewed. I knew the suave worship leader lived there too — I found him both cool and hot, and it was a wonder he was single. But I kept my cool while being interviewed by the housemates, who were busy assessing whether I was worthy of living in such a holy house. It wasn't until the end of the interview that Jake stepped in, popping in after worship practice. He was just as intimidating in person as he was in theory. He had the charisma of a boy band member, the looks of a celebrity, and the confidence of a lady's man.

Jake and I were good friends from the get-go. He knew about my struggle with same-sex attraction and asked me to be his accountability partner — someone you confided in when you were tempted to sin (or gave into temptation). Accountability partners met now and then, praying for each other and keeping each other accountable by asking how things were going. It made sense that we would become accountability partners since we lived together, even if he didn't struggle with homosexuality or sexual sin.

We also attended the same Bible college, and I learned immensely from his insight and perspective on interpretation. I quickly developed an inferiority complex when it came to him, constantly feeling small in the shadow of his greatness. I looked up to him and saw him as more than a brother in Christ; to me, our union was more intimate than what was shown on the surface. I shuddered at the thought of Jake being interested in me romantically and hated myself for thinking he'd be tempted in any way. However, I couldn't deny the effect he had on me; how my heart would flutter or stop for a second the moment he walked into a room or gave me one of his seductive smiles.

While Jake was certainly more flashy than a "normal" heterosexual man, I thought there was no way he was gay. I attributed anything I felt about him to my issue of same-sex attraction and decided to never share my feelings with him — I was afraid of making things awkward or distant. But the truth was there was always something more powerful going on between us, and I could never put my finger on it. So I just continued to be his friend and accountability partner and chalked up the chemistry to my sinful lust.

One night Jake pulled me aside and attributed a particular Bible verse to me, one that had been prescribed to him by his dad during his formative years. It seemed scripted yet seamless: a way for him to address my lack of stereotypically masculine traits as not being a product of homosexuality, but what the Bible called for: "*to be strong, act like a man, and observe what the Lord your God requires: walk in obedience to him, and keep his decrees and commands, his laws and regulations, as written in the Laws of Moses.*" I learned that this was my calling as a man struggling with same-sex attraction: to not worry about the world's view of what it means to be a man, but what God says it means to be a man. Moments like these were not infrequent, as Jake saw his duty to be some sort of role model to me.

This only complicated my feelings towards him - I felt he was a much better man than I, and I had much to learn from him. On the one hand, there was security in knowing we wouldn't be tempted in lust for each other; on the other, there always seemed to be unique chemistry between us. I constantly found myself in reckless obedience to him, like a timid dog to an alpha male. I wanted to be everywhere he was, and it seemed to be the same for him. I relished in the acknowledgment that he and I were some sort of dynamic duo, that we were, in many ways at that time, inseparable. It felt good to be close to another man without the temptation of sexual sin — a homosexual man can be friends with a seemingly heterosexual man. It was safe because there would never be temptation between us.

Or so I thought.

New Heights

It wasn't until the end of Jake's stay in the United States that our relationship began to take on a new form. Sure, we'd been classmates, running mates, accountability partners, housemates, and best friends, but that didn't seem to be enough. At the time, he was in a love relationship with the church secretary and constantly shared his struggles with their relationship with me. I'd offer to pray for him and be there when things got bad between them. He felt no sexual chemistry for this woman but did feel pressure to be with her, believing he was the problem by not listening to God's will.

Our talks bonded us even more, as he gained confidence in my confidentiality. We often stayed up late talking, and over several months, these nights turned into something more. They became a ritual Jake called "bro sessions." Once all our other roommates had gone to bed, Jake and I would stay behind to "talk," or if one of us had already retreated to his room, he'd sneak out to join the other.

It started slow — he'd caress my face and chest over my clothes, and I'd follow his lead. I remember the first time

Jake touched me. It sent shivers down my spine and electricity through my veins. This was a feeling I'd never felt before — one filled with excitement and tingling, a sense more powerful than any opioid. I wanted more but feared we'd be exposed and it would be blamed on me (because of my struggle with same-sex attraction). I could just hear it in my head: how the homosexual seduced the most kind-hearted, God-fearing man in the church. It would do me in, so I hid it as fiercely as my other sinful secrets. Jake did the same.

After the first time, I went to bed in awe, assuming it was a one-and-done situation. The following day, he and I woke up before the other housemates and met in the kitchen. He began lightly, but powerfully, touching my chest and arms as he glided on air by me, with the biggest smile on his face. I thought I was living a dream until one of our other housemates came out to join us. The touching and sensual glances stopped while the other housemate was there...and continued after he left. I wasn't sure what to make of it, so I trusted Jake's judgment and followed his lead. After all, it was the best feeling I had ever known.

As we continued this routine, I followed one rule to never advance further than him — to follow his lead. I kept reminding myself that *I* was the one who struggled with same-sex attraction; I was scared to push boundaries. The truth was, the situation left me perplexed. He was this all-loving, strong, confident, handsome worship leader. He could have any woman he wanted, but he chose to make me the object of his satisfaction. It felt amazing but was also the most confusing thing in my life. I didn't understand why someone wanted me in such an intimate way — especially a straight, godly man. I feared my homosexuality was more seductive than I'd imagined. Yet it soon became evident that this was his desire as well: he wanted to be with me and give such intimate pleasure and receive it.

Eventually, we graduated to more mature advances — under clothes. He felt my chest hair and caressed my nipples, and I did the same to him. The sessions got more intense as we explored each other's private parts. He first moved his fingers delicately down my body, from my chest to my feet, and back up again. Then he landed at my groin, his hand circling my erect shaft. I followed his lead, and it was evident that he was enjoying it, too.

When exploring my private parts, he touched everything from my butt to my balls but never past the base of my penis. We enjoyed each other's bodies, taking in the aroma of his pheromones given off from the sweat of his skin. We usually ended our sessions by holding each other close, trying to melt into each other's bodies. I remember the thoughts that ran through my brain when we held each other tightly. I constantly found myself the one gripping harder — a physical manifestation of my greatest emotional fears. Being held closely and tightly was all I'd ever wanted, and I feared that one day this would end. I wanted him to hold me forever, to be my everything.

I knew I could never put into words how I felt. It was a feeling I'd desired for so long, and it felt so right to experience this with another man. However, deep in my heart, I felt that what we were doing was wrong. Those times were most evident when he brought me to sexual climax against my control, and I found myself in the bathroom, cleaning up the mess. I'd look at myself in the mirror, saying things like, "*What have you done?*" "*Why are you so stupid?*" "*Couldn't you have controlled yourself? You're ruining it for both of you.*"

In my mind, I thought what we were doing was innocent, but I'd somehow found a way to make it sexual and disgusting. I thought bringing my struggle into the mix just made it worse for everyone. I was full of shame. Sometimes he'd stay until I cleaned up, and we'd continue; other times, he'd retreat to his bed for the night. The nights he fled were the ones I beat myself up about it the most.

This was the most sensual experience I'd ever had with a man up to this point. In my youth, I'd wrestled with guys in a way that stimulated me in specific ways, but this was different: it was mutually intimate. The advanced level of intimacy in our sessions continued for weeks — we found the time when our other housemates had gone to their rooms to have our private moments in the living room. Sometimes we were surprised by visitors; we'd immediately stop until they'd left but never talked about what we were doing.

Talking about our acts was a void between us. The need for secrecy wasn't lost on us, and we never talked about it with each other. It was like we had two different relationships: our public friendship and our secret love life. We had an understanding and connection that didn't need words or exposure (at least that's what I thought). So intimate and raw was our relationship that it lacked the need for words.

That is, until the last time.

Hard Knocks

Early one Saturday morning, the housemates were getting ready to attend the wedding of two fellow congregants. Jake was playing music at the service, so he had to go in early. I went with the rest of the housemates and met Jake there. At the reception after the service, Jake decided he needed to leave early to get ready to lead worship at church later that night. I decided to follow him home — I made up some excuse to leave early, but I just wanted to be around him. He was the only thing that felt comfortable at this time in my life.

Jake was leaving for Europe within a few months to help the senior pastor plant a church there (the term for establishing a new church in a new area), so significant changes were brewing. It had been announced that Ryan, the assistant pastor, would become the new senior pastor, and other leaders were shifting in their roles or going elsewhere. Jake's departure would leave a gaping hole not only in church leadership but also in my heart. He was leaving me soon, and I wanted to ensure I got as much time with him as possible.

We ended up in his room, on the bottom of his bunk bed. I laid on his lap, a pillow between my head and his crotch. I began stroking the back of his ear as he tenderly moved his hand up and down my back. The intimacy felt more potent, like the first time. I wondered if this was because of my feelings about him leaving soon or that our senses were even more alive (our first daytime session). Whatever it was, it felt special just to be with him.

After what felt like a fleeting moment, I heard a satisfactory sigh from him and thought he enjoyed my massage. Shortly after that, the aroma of his satisfaction became apparent – he had reached sexual climax. Although I speculated that other incidents during our sessions had made him finish, this was the most obvious: I could smell it. I thought nothing of it until he said he needed to take a shower and get ready — a few hours before his commitments later that evening. The look of concern on his face was evident and made me feel uncomfortable. I wanted badly to ask if everything was OK but found myself in a state of shock. I was then politely asked to leave.

Later that night, after church, I got a text from Jake asking me to meet him downstairs to go for a ride to the shore. He started with niceties — telling me about his day and how the Lord had worked through him during the service.

Eventually, he got to the subject of his request.

He'd conversed with his mother about our "bro sessions," and they'd determined that a discussion needed to be had with me. To what extent he told his mom of our intimacy is still a mystery to me. I couldn't imagine a mother hearing about how her angel of a son had taken part in such sinful debauchery unless details had been left out...or were painted as deceitful coercion on my part. I vacillated between those two possibilities for years as I pondered my predicament: I was the one who struggled with homosexuality, who was caught seducing the star member of the church. Paranoia filled my mind often and fueled my most profound shame and insecurities.

His lecture didn't make matters any better. The way he described the situation made it clear that he thought the reason things had advanced as far as they had was because of my struggle. Even though I'd followed my rule not to go any further than he did, and he'd always been the one to initiate, I still felt the burden of responsibility since I was the one who struggled with same-sex attraction.

My fear of word getting out spiked at that moment — after all, his mother now knew of the situation. I was afraid I'd be seen as taking advantage of his kindness and manipulating him to partake in sexual sin. This paranoia wasn't far from reality — women who were sexually harassed in the church were constantly seen as the antagonist. The belief was that what they wore or how they flirted attracted the men to them, causing men to "stumble." I feared this could be seen as the case for me, given my struggle with same-sex attraction. I could be seen as having given in to temptation and lured a heterosexual man into my sin.

I sat in silence as Jake told me that this type of behavior was customary in his household — his family had cuddle sessions frequently, so it wasn't unusual to him. At that moment, it didn't occur to me the weight of that admission, but if his family did engage in such acts, it was child abuse and molestation. What we did wasn't innocent; it was a mutual, consensual expression of lust. Yet, the theme of his discussion was that the fault was mine, and I started to get defensive.

He said he'd forgotten to consider my struggle with "same-sex attraction" and that he felt remorse for not being conscious of my struggle before engaging in these sessions with me. I was the problem — I was the one with a struggle that needed to be restrained, not nurtured. In his words, our intimacy sessions were a "stumbling block" to me, and for that, he was sorry. I tried to protest — to justify the acts we'd committed together. My attempt to explain why we did what we did only seemed to backfire. Looking back, it was as if I was trying to redeem a failed relationship, reviving it from the brink of death. I knew what we were doing was wrong within the context of the church, but I also knew that in my heart, it felt right. I wanted what we had to live.

He continued. He was months away from leaving the country to help start a church across the globe, and the last thing he needed was this distraction. Not long before our conversation, he'd broken up with the church secretary and taken an interest in a new lover — a woman he said he was pursuing as a potential spouse. This was a real low point for me. To cover up his transgressions and nurture the confidence of secrecy, I'd obliged his requests of confidentiality to show my support of his new life. After all, in my mind, it was the least I could do, considering my struggle had become his burden.

I couldn't move or speak — I felt like a piece of shit. The shell of a man I was became even more hollow as I heard how my affliction had caused him so much grief. I also felt immense shame that I'd been exposed. Even after all the years of "praying the gay away," going through conversion therapy and counseling, and suppressing my desires (except for watching gay porn), my affliction had ended one of the most intimate relationships I'd ever experienced. I felt both a sense of defeat and a new admiration for the man who made my affliction the cause of our dysfunction.

I agreed with him, saying I understood his concerns. I apologized for my transgressions. He lit up, telling me how much of a blessing it had been that I recognized my errors and that we would no longer partake in such activities. A burst of joy filled his face as he thanked me profusely for understanding his predicament and perspective. I vowed to never speak about it or to engage in such shameful acts. It took me years to realize just how much my "transgression" was a cover-up, a cloak for the shame of his insecurities.

Journal Entry: Tuesday, April 20, 2010

*Partial Entry

...the talk with [Jake] was awkward, but good. I knew it was going to happen, but the way he addressed it really showed characteristics of a real man. He was loving and addressed the issue of sin it really was. My insecurities kicked in as I tried to interpret what "he really was trying to say." I felt super awkward about the whole thing, but I pray the Lord will give me better words to say. There were some really sinful aspects of the situation I am deathly afraid to admit, but as the Lord leads. I got quiet but responded [internally] with many filters & analyzations of my thoughts. I feel I wasn't as truthful as I should have been, but I don't know how much of it was to protect him vs my embarrassment. Lord, please lead me in my words. I know how weak & awkward I am in regard to confrontation.

CHAPTER

12

DROPS IN THE BUCKET

When things ended with Jake, my heart was broken. I filled my time supporting him as best I could after he got settled in Europe. I joined his missionary team, helping him raise funds in the U.S. and keeping the local church up to date on his happenings. This gave me a sense of purpose and closeness to him. We video-messaged each other now and then to catch up on life, and I relayed the news I got from him to the church, talking about all the great things he was doing to advance the gospel of Jesus abroad.

I felt a void in my life and longed to fill it with purpose and meaning. But, unfortunately, Kristina had gone to Europe to plant the new church, as well, which made the vacuum of loneliness even more powerful. Amid these complex feelings, I decided to reach out to my old work friend Alexis to catch up on life.

Planting the Seed

Alexis and I had been like two peas in a pod at work. We'd met at the retail store I'd worked at during college, and she often worked the register while I collected shopping carts outside. Every time she saw me come in for a break, she made intense eye contact and sometimes loud bird calls. The supervisors resented her; she was constantly pulled into the office for performance issues and even written up a couple of times. Tenacious and brilliant, she didn't care — she felt free to be herself, which drew me to her even more. We were the same age, and her confidence enamored me. Getting to know her made her even more of an anomaly to me, as I sought my own identity.

We also partied hard together. She remembers a night at my sister's house when we were all playing beer pong with our coworkers in the garage. She and her other friend were watching me (apparently, the friend had told Alexis she should try to hook up with me that night). Just as Alexis was about to make a move, I made drunken eye contact with her from across the table and cleared the cups in one ridiculous swoop. Apparently, I had done something in a way that revealed my hidden sexuality because I made Alexis laugh but also had her wonder whether I was even interested in women. She retreated from her advances, and we continued to party on.

One day she informed me that she'd decided to leave the area to pursue her acting career in Los Angeles. I was bummed by the news (yet another loss) but knew she and I lived completely different lives. Even though I'd built my life in the church, it was hard to hear that she was leaving, considering all we had been through. Her pursuits and priorities were different from mine; she represented my "old nature." She was the only person with whom I'd stayed in contact from my party days; most of my friends had moved on once I'd become an Evangelical pastor. Who could blame them? I was an outspoken Jesus freak who condemned them for things I'd once done with them.

We decided to meet downtown for Thai food so I could hear about her plans. I was also excited to talk to her about potential new opportunities at the church. I was holy-rolling, telling her how great life was, how much I enjoyed my new Christian housemates, and how I'd decided to enroll in Bible college. I told her about the European church plant and how many people had moved on, creating space for new leaders on the church leadership team. I could tell she was a bit surprised but supportive, nonetheless. Finally, she filled me in on her latest adventure in Los Angeles — she'd applied for a transfer to the local retail store there and was pursuing her bachelor's degree.

I felt courage well up within me — I wanted to share what the Lord was doing in my life concerning my sexuality. I desperately looked for a good moment in our conversation to bring up the topic of my testimony — because I considered her a dear friend and wanted to tell her about my relationship with Jesus. When I got to the part about my struggle with same-sex attraction, I assured her I sought deliverance from this sexual sin. It was as if all the air had been sucked out of the room as I tried to find a way to explain what I was talking about. It was my understanding and experience that secular people didn't understand how Jesus can "heal homosexuality," but there was something that felt different revealing this to Alexis. After finishing my explanation, she gave me one of the most honest looks of love and concern I'd ever seen and said simply, "I'm sad for you."

This took me by surprise. I'd received similar responses before from nonbelievers, but her tone and concern took me aback. Rarely did I feel a sense of love and compassion for my situation, as most people regarded me as a nutjob. On the other hand, Alexis showed genuine concern for my beliefs about myself and was unreserved in sharing that. I told her there was nothing to be sad about, that Jesus would heal me of my affliction.

She wasn't buying it. A free-thinking liberal, she knew what she wanted even though she was still finding herself. Nevertheless, the look on her face never left me — to this day, it's seared in my mind. In hindsight, that moment was the beginning of the end of my search to "heal" my same-sex attraction. Her genuine concern was like nothing

I knew in or out of the church because it was born of genuine care and concern for my wellbeing. It was also the first time homosexuality was presented to me in a good light by someone who genuinely cared about me.

She didn't hide behind a multi-thousand-year-old book to have me deny who I was; she wanted to see me liberated, happy, and free. I didn't know what to say; at the time, I just chalked it up to her "being lost" and "not understanding the ways of the Lord." This was my typical response to such pushback, but the memory of her body language lingered.

Our conversation may have ended on an awkward note, but our friendship was revived later in life. We reconnected when I made my way to Los Angeles, and we've been friends ever since.

Starting a New Chapter

My heart didn't stay broken for long, as I was allowed to form a new identity as a leader. When the senior pastor left for Europe with a whole group of people to plant a church, the then-assistant pastor Ryan took the helm. Ryan was recruiting his leadership team, and I was on the shortlist; he asked to meet to discuss his vision.

I was excited about the possibilities. I knew I did every-thing right according to the non-existent, God-forsaken handbook of church obedience. I'd committed my life to the faith so literally that I'd abandoned my aspirations for "worldly things" (become an accountant to make money and find pleasure in the things of life). I'd made quite the impression on leadership, dating back to my door-greeting days and Bible study group. I'd forsaken all I knew for this church, so I figured it was time for me to reap the rewards of my sacrifices.

After meeting with Ryan about the roles he had in mind for me, I was less than pleased to hear that I'd be in charge of outreach, in addition to my duties with high school min-istry. It wasn't that I didn't enjoy outreach, but I thought my efforts in the youth group made me the ideal candidate for the youth pastor role. The youth pastor was also taking on more responsibilities but would continue in his posi-tion.

I didn't let my disappointment show; instead, I grate-fully accepted the offer. I was told I'd receive a monthly salary of $300, but I politely declined the money since I was already working a full-time job in the mornings and thought the money would be better used in the new en-deavors of the church. This worked out great for me. I was able to do my morning job and head to the church to do my volunteer job. Life couldn't have been sweeter.

I attended weekly staff meetings when I could but mainly was conferenced in or told about it by other leadership members since sessions always seemed to happen when I was working. I was thrilled to be part of the team — I could finally get a behind-the-scenes look at how the church operated. The group consisted of people who'd been there for quite some time, but we all approached it with a new vision since this was a new endeavor. At least that's what I thought at the time.

Becoming a Pastor

It was customary for the leadership team to go on an annual retreat to encourage team-building and promote visioning. Our first retreat was held in the mountains of Northern California at a cabin owned by a church member. I instantly felt like an outsider when I witnessed everyone's comfort with one another as they joked and made puns together. I closely watched what I said, wondering who I was to be amongst such holiness. Ryan was revered as God-ordained; he embodied the vision for the church. Just as the man was the head of the household, so was the senior pastor to the church (they claimed Jesus was the head of the church, but it actually was just the senior pastor).

What made this retreat so memorable was what happened one specific afternoon. I was walking with the leadership team after we'd completed individual devotionals. I felt strongly that I didn't belong – they all knew each other and had many inside jokes and stories. I felt awkward until the conversation turned to business. Ryan was getting accolades for his new position, and if there was anything I knew I was good at, it was buttering up the egos of others. I don't recall the content of my affirmations, but it ended with me receiving a few of my own from Ryan.

This was the first time the title "pastor" was assigned to me, and I felt exceptional. I never thought I would see the day that I, too, would become a pastor. Ryan told me my role was just as important as his. I'd be a pastor to the unsaved; my position would be necessary for recruiting lost sheep to the church. "Outreach Pastor" had a great ring to it, and from that day forward, I decided to pour my heart and soul into generating numbers for the church.

This was a turning point. I found a new identity in being a pastor of outreach. I vowed on that trip that I would set an excellent example in this newly-created position. I spent the rest of the trip jotting down thoughts about the different ministries I'd create.

Getting to Work

I made myself an office in the overflow room at the church and began working feverishly on my personal computer. The staff didn't set me up like they had the other pastors at the church. I had to use my own equipment and email address. I was also curious about why I wasn't already on the church website but happy I was at least on the bulletin board at the church entrance. But that didn't deter me from my vision and determination. I wrote out a list of ideas for upcoming events: Christmas Week, movie nights, fellowship potlucks, concerts — you name it! I was determined to prove myself in this new role and created subcommittees and chairs to oversee these endeavors. The church was putting on a new face, and I was the one to control it all.

I wasted no time in getting my plans underway. There'd never been an outreach pastor before, but since it was necessary to Ryan, he'd carved it out (hoping that I'd fulfill it to his liking). I planned multiple events and ministries, such as starting our first-ever elderly home visits and homeless outreach. I also created a prison ministry, where we went to the local juvenile hall to share Jesus with inmates who were minors. However, my most prized accomplishment was creating an entire week of events for Christmas, all centered around outreach and preaching Jesus to people. Ryan was ecstatic at my zeal and commitment to the position.

Ryan and I met weekly. Half our time was spent on business, the other on personal matters. He told me he wanted to disciple me (help me grow in my faith). He had a vested interest in me as a person and leader, and I couldn't have been more honored. I started looking up to him as a father figure, sharing more about my life than what was probably comfortable for him to hear. He seemed very interested in my well-being initially, so it was easy for me to open up about my struggles.

I shared with him my struggles with homosexuality, finding refuge in admitting my sins and temptations. Where Jake was once my accountability partner, Ryan seemed to take over (except without physical touch). He asked if I wanted to put him down as the accountability partner to my internet search history for a software program that reported suspicious content to a designated person, a decision I reluctantly accepted for fear he would see my scandalous sin if I slipped on my roundabout way of looking at porn. The last thing I needed him to see was my search history. It was OK, though, because I had an old iPhone that I used for porn instead.

He also took a strong interest in my romantic life and was curious about my dating habits. This topic was usually quick and easy: I had none. I knew it was a bad look to be a struggling homosexual and not have found heterosexual love yet. This was a concern expressed to me in orchestrating my first and only female relationship (more on that soon).

Turning Tides

About a year into my pastoral role, things started to take a turn. I started suggesting significant changes to the way things were done around the church, and others became skeptical of my motives and aspirations. Since I had the ear of the man in charge, I could rock the boat, and specific individuals were intimidated by my rise to fame. The criticism started slowly; I got backhanded compliments about my work and heard whisperings from second-hand sources about certain people's displeasure with my status.

That said, it wasn't until Ryan's mother and sister moved to the area that shit began to hit the fan. Even as women in a church notorious for its misogynistic ideals (among many other things), it was evident that they wielded quite a bit of power. Their presence and participation became more common as they sat in on prayer meetings and volunteered for events I chaired. They signed up as co-chairs on many of my subcommittees and weren't afraid to give me feedback on leadership techniques (gleaned from their own failed attempts to start a coffee business in the area).

I cherished their friendship, thinking they were looking out for my best interests. They shared seemingly sensitive information that I assumed Ryan had told them about the inner workings of the church. However, once revered as a great example of intimacy, this friendship soon morphed into something much more conniving and deceitful. They pried information about others in the church, which I provided, thinking they were considerate individuals who just wanted to be more plugged in to a community to which they were new.

Eventually, I put their friendship to the test by revealing information I said was private; when it came back around to me, I knew my suspicions were correct. From then on, I knew I had to watch my words with these women — everything I told them would ultimately get back to Ryan, but with a manipulative spin. The sweet, cookie-baking persona was stripped away as I saw the cunning nature underneath. They were the ears of a leader who I'd come to find was a much weaker man than he portrayed through his collection of alpha male activities.

My suspicions were also aroused by a change in Ryan's tone and character. Where our weekly meetings had once felt like father-son bonding sessions, they were now energetically cloudy, and I wondered about his view of me. This started slowly; I thought he was just feeling the pressure of filling the shoes of the former pastor (once regarded as one of the best teachers of the Bible in the Christian community). But things started to change between us, and our meetings became shorter and less intimate.

The meetings eventually became strictly business. He slowly disregarded the portion dedicated to my personal life; he said he was too busy to talk or asked me to speak to someone else about my issues. I became suspicious and desperate for someone to talk to. I felt incredibly alone in my struggle after losing two of the most important people in my life to Europe. Now, after a year of what had felt like fatherly nurturing, Ryan had no time for my personal life.

Little did I know that the boats being rocked were caused by a hurricane he was looking to avoid.

PART

4

CRUCIFIXION

GORDON

Gordon was your stereotypical gothic Christian. Black was his favorite color; it only took a few weeks of knowing him to see that his wardrobe was composed entirely of black t-shirts and black cargo pants. Gordon would've been the perfect cult leader had he developed a personality and tolerance for people. He was always the most intelligent guy in the room (or at least, he effectively convinced everyone of that). Multiple people who I idolized said Gordon was a genius. Even as my Bible school teacher, this brilliance was yet to be uncovered, but I pressed on in the narrative to appease my idols.

Gordon and I had a bizarre relationship. We met in the men's Bible study he co-led, and at the time, he was both the missionary pastor and Bible college leader. Our first encounter wasn't memorable — all I remember was that our body language seemed to express from the beginning that we never really liked each other. Of course, this was strictly unspoken; we never said how we felt about each other in words. But the tensions between us became more relevant when he assumed the role of assistant pastor.

Looking back now, I can't blame Gordon. Here I was, this loud, gregarious, closeted homosexual who, after being given designer rights by Ryan, set out to Fab 5 the church he thought to be his fortress. Shortly after Ryan assumed the senior pastor position, he and I walked through the church sanctuary to discuss desperately needed alterations. The previous pastor didn't have an eye for design, nor did he care to keep the church sanctuary up to date with the latest trends. Gordon was at the piano, practicing for worship, and was visibly annoyed with us (specifically me). As Ryan and I approached the stage to assess the curtains, Gordon angrily spat at me, "You know this isn't [Real Life Church]!" I was shocked — not at what he'd said, but that he actually had a voice of his own, and it manifested in a passive-aggressive way.

I knew Ryan listened to Gordon and could tell that Ryan was torn between the two of us on several issues. I had reason to believe that there were plenty of topics discussed behind closed doors that Gordon found egregious. On countless occasions, Ryan sat down with me to discuss my behavior – i.e., letting the high school kids listen to Taylor Swift (Gordon said she was a harlot); dancing and singing to a provocative rap song with the high schoolers (Gordon saw a video posted on social media by one of the high schoolers and complained to Ryan), and other ridiculous accusations. Although Ryan appeared to be the head of the church, Gordon seemed to be the brain.

Starting Afresh

I knew the tension between Gordon and me needed to be resolved. After all, he was now second-in-command and had the love and respect of Ryan. So I decided to try allowing Gordon to see my vulnerable side. Plus, the incident with Jake was eating at me more intensely; I felt the weight of being a pastor and needed to talk to someone about it.

After my discussion with Jake, my belief that I was the problem got more intense. I kept telling myself Jake was innocent, and the stimulation resulted from my sin and required repenting. Enough time had passed since Jake left for Europe that I decided it was OK to share my experience with someone finally, and I thought it would be a moment of truce to share it with Gordon.

I started cautiously, telling him I needed to talk to him about some sinful acts I'd committed with another man. I tried to use discrete words, but even a baboon would've known who I was talking about. I made sure to keep the focus on me, not to place any blame upon Jake. I shared that we'd had late-night "bro sessions where we went beyond cuddling and admitted that it aroused me. I told him I felt shame about what we'd done and that the blame was all my own. I told him my struggle with same-sex attraction seemed to be the culprit and that I needed forgiveness for my sins.

I could tell he was instantly uncomfortable. He wasn't someone who liked confrontation, or emotions, or humans. He looked at me in shock, a deer in headlights (not unusual for him). He then swiveled his chair around to stare up at the ceiling. This didn't surprise me, as this was his usual reaction when giving advice. Gordon was notorious for being distant and vague. He constantly gave "advice" followed by a neutral Bible verse or story to absolve him of the responsibility of explicitly approving or disapproving of something. I walked out of his office more confused than affirmed but made sure to stroke his ego in telling him how much I appreciated his ear and prayer.

Honestly, sharing with Gordon was strictly strategic. I needed some clout with him, desperately needing his approval, and I thought being open and honest would put me in his good graces. I knew this would be no easy feat, so I pressed on to somehow please him.

Seeking Approval

It was clear Ryan was getting tired of my woes around my relationship with Sarah, a woman I'd begun seeing essentially at his behest. Our weekly meetings started to be taken up by my struggles in the relationship with her — a relationship that lasted for eight long months. Ryan was a large part of why we were together (more on that shortly), so I felt he could advise. Eventually, however, Ryan gave up — he went away on a pastor's retreat and handed the emotional burden to Gordon.

I wasn't excited about Gordon being my confidant, but here we were — it was him or no one. The fact that I was willing to talk to Gordon about this indicated how bad things got with Sarah. I sought him out for advice, hoping once again that my vulnerability would ease the tension between us; my insatiable desire to be liked extended to this toxic, stoic character. I knew deep down how I felt about my relationship with Sarah — that it didn't sit well with me. I was at my wits' end; it felt like metal grinding metal trying to make it work. I was convinced it was her — her presence was simply an annoyance that ate me alive.

Gordon now bore the brunt of these weekly crisis meetings and was not feeling it. He never gave me straightforward advice. Instead, he punted me to a vague Bible verse and left me to my own conclusions. I constantly had to form my own opinion on what he was advising me to do. Not having a brain or spine of my own at the time, I interpreted his advice as a wise choice to break up with her, so I did.

His constant elusiveness was a set-up since blame could never be pinned on him for leading someone astray. He was thus always free to lambast the person for making the "wrong decision." He avoided confrontation at any cost...until it was clear he'd be able to nail someone to the cross for what he saw as their violation of the Bible.

Crusades

As soon as I ended things with Sarah, Gordon came for blood. It was as if he'd let the dogs out and was hell-bent on a conviction. He had more closed-door meetings with Ryan in an apparent attempt to stage an ambush on me as he'd once done with Jake.

I vividly remembered a crusade Gordon had spearheaded to shame and punish Jake after breaking up with the church secretary. Gordon claimed Jake had led her on in their relationship (Gordon was notorious for riding Bible verses and legalism into the ground). As the Bible college leader, Gordon had an arsenal of verses and interpretations at his disposal. I wasn't sure which rules Jake had broken, but whatever they were, they incensed Gordon, and he was out for blood. At the time, this took me by surprise because if anyone sang the praises of Gordon, it was Jake. They'd appeared to be the best of friends, but it had ended in an all-out war.

I learned from this event and didn't want a repeat performance when I broke up with Sarah. My concerns about Gordon's crusades weren't irrational. As militant as he was on his view of women conforming to "God's intended purpose of women," Gordon seemed to have a strange affection for the women in the church and fiercely condemned the men who broke their hearts. It was clear that Gordon was both passive-aggressive and vengeful, and it would soon be my turn to bear the brunt of it. Just as Gordon and Ryan had teamed up to try to have Jake removed from the European leadership team (Gordon had persuaded Ryan to join his crusade), he came for me as if I had never consulted with him about breaking it off with Sarah.

He instantly turned on me, just like with Jake. However, unlike what happened with Jake, Ryan took me under his wing and shielded me from Gordon's wrath. I still don't know whether this was because Ryan felt guilty for fixing up a homosexual man with a woman, handing me off to Gordon to talk about it, feeling guilty about how he'd come after Jake in the past, or something else, but I knew I was being treated differently than in times past.

Misogyny at its Finest

Bayside was notorious for conforming to gender roles, and if misogyny had a representative within the organization, it was Gordon. If the subject of a woman's place being in the home and church were a team sport, he would've been the coach, team captain, and cheerleader. His ultra-conservative views of women were no mystery to anyone, as he preached about them anywhere he could. Whether he was teaching a Bible college class or filling in for Ryan for church services, he made sure to slip in some sexist verse. His wife was a meek, charming woman who never spoke out of turn. Whether that was her actual personality or forced upon her by the man in her life, she fit the mold of Gordon's proclivities.

If it weren't my failed relationship with Sarah that would do me in with Gordon, it would be how I supposedly exploited other women in the church. For example, towards the end of my relationship with Sarah, I started a Christian clothing company. This was a way for me to express multiple passions at once: business, graphic design, and preaching the gospel. That was quite literally the company's name: Preach the Gospel 316 (316 referring to a famous verse in the Bible that outlines the salvation message, John 3:16). The company was short-lived. I traveled to trade shows and Christian concerts to sell t-shirts that conveyed Bible verses in images and text. I had envisioned different designs, but with a limited budget, I couldn't keep up with the inventory. I thought I'd wind things down until the local Christian bookstore asked me to sell my shirts there.

This was huge! I needed new marketing materials, so I asked my male roommate with attractive features and a couple of women in the church to be models for my clothing line. I had my friend assist me, shooting photos around downtown, wearing my shirts. It was great; the models were beautiful, and they showed off my brand brilliantly. However, this offended Gordon, and I was given a stern lecture to stop exploiting women and causing men to stumble.

By this point, I'd had enough of Gordon's passive aggression, so I did what I thought was the best Christian thing to do — take counsel. I emailed Ryan for his opinion, the result of which was that I'd continue to do what I'd been doing, and Gordon would just have to deal with it. This was just another point of tension between Gordon and me, but I wasn't going to sit it out anymore. So I avoided him like the plague after that, which was hard since he was my Bible teacher.

Email: Me to Pastor Ryan
Date: July 31, 2011
Subject: Need your opinion...

Hey Pastor [Ryan]!

I wanted to run something by you and get your opinion on it. I was asked by Pastor [Gordon] to cease taking model pictures of the women specifically in our church in order to prevent their exploitation as well as to prevent men from stumbling. I wanted to get your opinion on this and see if you were in agreeance with this due the fact that I have had quite a few gals in our fellowship ask me if they could be shirt models. I would need to respond appropriately to them if it is the case that the church is not ok with this. My response to them would be that I was asked by leadership not to have ladies from our fellowship be models and leaving it at that. However, I would not want to speak on behalf of the entire church if this is not a church decision and is an individual conviction. I don't mean any form of dissension from this and will respect Pastor [Gordon]'s conviction on this subject by ceasing from taking any lady model pictures until the Lord gives me further clarity on it. Thank you and God bless you!!!

*email chain

Pastor [Ryan]: Let's hook up in the next couple days and talk.

Me: Cool...I'm leaving early wed morning for SWC...if you can't meet up before, no worries, after works for me!

It's not a big deal & I hear his heart in it...

Pastor [Ryan]: cool, just fyi this is not a leadership thing, I haven't had an issue with it at all, I didn't know about it before, but would still love to talk to you anyway.
:)

SARAH

I was happy and content, living my best life as the out-reach pastor in the first few months. I was shaping the ministry to my liking and recruiting a steady group of helpers. I'd formed friendships with the few people my age at Bayside and kept a healthy distance from women as per the church's guidelines. Everything seemed great in my life; I had no room for distractions.

During a weekly meeting with Ryan, we turned to a personal topic. He asked how I was doing and whether I was finding time to date. I told him I was busy and happy with the ministry, with no time to do anything of the sort. Deep down, I was ecstatic that I had a distraction from dating — I couldn't imagine what it would be like to date a woman. Although I wasn't fully healed from same-sex attraction, I wasn't tempted to act on it, so I felt I was in a good place and didn't need to entertain the idea of dating a woman. Ryan's inquiry wasn't strange, but it made me suspicious.

It was odd being a single Christian man in this church. At the "old" age of 23, I was still without a wife (or suitable match). After rumors had circulated a couple of years before Kristina and I were secret lovers (and leadership's discomfort in seeing us so close without a romantic commitment), I made sure that none of my female friendships looked anything like that. I didn't need another lecture from leadership, telling me how my closeness with women painted the wrong image. I figured it was best to follow the rules and let things be.

However, people from church were curious about my sexuality. At that point, plenty of people knew I struggled with same-sex attraction, which set the imaginations of some ablaze. How was it that I was so involved and still couldn't find a match? I was the ideal bachelor — single, relatively handsome, charismatic, and devoted to God. Being a pastor without a wife and struggling with same-sex attraction was not a cute look in this church. This eventually caught the attention of Ryan, who made sure to mention it.

It was apparent when there was a buzz around the church. Typically, congregants first talked amongst themselves, then strategically hid a topic of interest in the form of a prayer request or concern. If someone of influence were involved, it would eventually make its way to Ryan, who'd then decide whether to address it with the person of concern. I could tell this topic was up in one of our weekly meetings. Ryan brought up the subject of dating again, asking whether I'd given any thought to what we'd spoken about last time. I told him nothing had changed and that I was still just focusing on the ministry.

He proceeded to tell me about Daisy, a girl in the church who was smitten with me. My constant involvement with her had some wondering about my interest in her. Ryan's wife was mentoring Daisy, and it was evident that she was forming feelings for me. When I told Ryan the feelings weren't mutual, it raised concerns about my single state (again). He made it vividly clear that someone with my stature in the church was an anomaly, especially considering my struggle — and that it didn't look good. Then, he doubled down by stating that it was about time I considered a suitor to squander such suspicions.

Arranged Derangement

The weekly meetings with Ryan eventually became a kind of ChristianMingle.com forum, except the suitable bachelorettes were the scarce array of available women in the church. Ryan consistently highlighted specific single women, and I always found a reason to object. I didn't want to participate in such conversations, but I knew this was important to my future leadership endeavors and appeasing Ryan.

I also recognized that this could be the next step to healing from same-sex attraction, so I obliged. We eventually settled on someone who appeared a perfect match (as perfect as a woman could be for a gay man). Sarah was intelligent, quiet, and, most importantly, obedient. She had a job and was the right age — she'd soon want to get married and have kids. It just made sense.

Thus ensued an awkward period of me trying to court Sarah. Where conversations with Ryan were once filled with ministry-related topics, they were now filled with coaching and counseling on courting and dating. I knew in my soul that the whole thing didn't feel right but thought this was what I needed to do. So, I started in group settings, inviting her to game nights and getting one-on-one time with her. Eventually, I asked her to be my girlfriend, thinking that would ease the tension of awkwardness I felt deep down. Little did I know it would only make things worse.

Talk of Marriage

Two weeks after Sarah and I started dating, discussions with Ryan got more intense. Sarah and I barely knew each other — we'd only really hung out at youth group. We had different groups of friends, and already Ryan was asking me about marriage. *"If you believe God has brought you together, why are you waiting to pop the question?"* I found every excuse in the book to evade the marriage questions while simultaneously wondering why I felt so much resistance to dating her. I felt like I was crawling out of my skin, not knowing what I was doing dating a woman.

I told Ryan I was concerned about living expenses, so he gave me examples of his union, saying that had he waited until the right time to marry his wife, they would've never gotten married. After responding to my every excuse, I began to believe God had put me with Sarah to teach me how to be selfless — to learn how to put her needs before mine. There were plenty of examples of arranged (and deranged) marriages in the Bible, so why was I any different? It was the only explanation I could come up with for the discomfort I felt in our relationship.

I felt like a floundering fish in meetings with Ryan, which began to be almost daily. Eventually, I mustered up the courage to ask Ryan why I felt the way I did. He chalked it up to my dual natures — the new self and the old self. The new self (i.e., my new creation in Christ) knew being with Sarah was the right thing to do, but the old self (i.e., my homosexual self) was rearing its ugly head to destroy what was ordained.

The analogy of feeding the two dogs became a staple of our conversations — the concept that I had the choice to feed one or the other, and whichever I fed would become the strongest. My new nature needed to be fed by the scriptures, praying, and meditations before the Lord, while my old nature needed to be starved to death. As much as I tried, though, I couldn't kick the feeling that something wasn't right.

One night I decided to take Sarah down to the water's edge and share my "testimony." We had an awkward dinner and made our way down to the docks. I loved this spot — it was where I paused on nightly runs to take in the beauty of the ocean and nature around it. We sat on the dock as I cuddled her close. I told her how I struggled with same-sex attraction and that our union had been a difficult one for me. I quoted scripture to help ease the moment's tension, but it didn't seem to help. It was like trying to walk in shoes that were too big; I fumbled over words and phrases, feeling like I was stomping on eggshells.

Eventually, the conversation came around to the topic of marriage (mind you, we'd been dating for less than a month at this point). I thought maybe this would be the trick — that if I were to commit at some point, my uncomfortable feelings would go away, and I'd be able to live as my new self! I brought up the desire to one day propose to her but that my struggle with homosexuality has been too hard to make such a commitment so early in the relationship. Again, I was the problem. I promised her that it would happen one day, not realizing the weight of that conversation and how she longed for such a union with a man she loved.

This took place around the holidays, and we each made separate plans with our families. That year my family had Thanksgiving at my sister's house, which was in the neighboring town. I pulled my sister aside to let her know I was thinking about popping the question to Sarah soon and how God wanted me to at some point. She looked at me blankly and didn't know what to say. Finally, she tried to smooth it over by changing the subject — a typical response when she disapproved of a choice but didn't want to overreact. This had me second-guess my confidence. The truth was, she embodied how I felt; her instincts reflected what I was suffering myself.

Coming Out of the Wilderness

Months went by, and things just seemed to get worse. Towards the end, it seemed that Sarah's insecurities were constantly triggered by mine. We found it a struggle to be around each other, as I resorted to watching gay porn even more than before (but never told her or anyone about it). Trying to love her became a burden, something to be endured (something I once told her — a share that didn't go over well).

I constantly found myself stressed out by the idea of one day having to propose, especially after the commitment I'd made to her that night out on the dock.

After months of this, I broke the news to her after Saturday night service that I needed a break — I needed time to pray about our relationship. This took her by surprise, and she burst into tears. I had no idea what to do. We decided to take a 6-week break to figure out the trajectory of our relationship. The following day at Sunday service was a bit awkward, but I felt a moment of relief. That is until I received an email from Sarah the night after the start of our break:

Email: Sarah to me
Date: June 26, 2011
Subject: (no subject)

Hi George,

There are a few things that I want you to know going into these next 6 weeks.

First, thank you again for your apology today, and I am sorry that I've shared too much without first seeking you on that.

I want you to know that I'm not giving up and fleeing. If I'm being honest with us both, what you've shared with me is not too much [same-sex attraction]. Nothing is too big for God to deal with and to work through. You've shared honestly and I recognize and appreciate that you've worked at being vulnerable. I want to work through this with you, and to help you through this in God's will. I'm not scared to work through those things with you and it does not intimidate me. I know that there are a lot of scars and they need time to heal and I pray for both of us that this time wouldn't be about being independent and "single" but that it would be an opportunity for each of us to focus on what the Lord is teaching us and needs to do in us as individuals.

I also want to let you know that my intention during this time is to interact with you as a brother. I do not intend to avoid you or to ignore you. I understand that there must be space and distance during this time and I intend to be humble and respectful to you. That being said, I do want to let you know that this morning when I first came into the coffee house I was not ignoring you or avoiding you. I had a situation that needed immediate attention and was in need of getting it taken care of.

> I'm not expecting nor do I need a response to these things, but wanted to let you know.
>
> I pray God will bless you abundantly during this time and show you His everlasting grace and mercy and that He works mightily in your life for you solely to bring you closer to Him.
>
> -[Sarah]

I didn't know what to say. I was at a loss for words at the thought of her endurance in this relationship. I knew that our 6-week break was six weeks too long. After pondering her words, I reached out to Ryan for help. I was desperate and needed advice. Instead, he punted me to Gordon. After an awkward and extremely vague meeting with Gordon (where I was forced to read between the lines of his advice), I felt it was right to call things off:

> **Email**: me to Sarah
> **Date**: June 27, 2011
> **Subject**: (no subject)
>
> Hey [Sarah],
>
> Thank you for the email. I totally agree and believe we confirmed on Saturday night that our interactions are to be that of brotherly/sisterly conduct.

As far as our situation, I want to let you know something to not invoke any false sense of hope. As far as us being together, unless the Lord makes it miraculously clear otherwise, I believe that our relationship as a couple will not continue. After our talk on Saturday, I realized that the issue is more than my struggles I shared with you [same-sex attraction]. Our inability to relate consists of our incompatibility and lack of trust in each other. Considering the makeup of our relationship these past 7 months, I have realized that we are trying to make something work that just won't by trying to nullify who God created us to be as individuals in our personalities. Our union should be natural and organically administered by the Holy Spirit & our gears grinding only justifies the reason for this relationship to be ended. Yes, there are things we lay down to the Lord for each other, but to try to change our personalities and even to the point of our identities in the Lord is not that which we are called to surrender. This, I have realized, is what we are doing and we must come to the realization that this is not what we are to be in our relationship.

I don't want you to be someone you are not because that will only make you and me miserable, nor do I for myself. The Lord has created you to be you and to ask for something different would only be in opposition of the beautiful creation God has made you to be. In a relationship, I have come to realize that our personalities should be recognized and synchronized harmonically through the Holy Spirit and this has very clearly not been the case.

Like I said Saturday night, I completely believe the Lord called us to this relationship. As far as it's duration, I am convinced our season is over. I know you will make an amazing wife because you exemplify that character of a Proverbs 31 women and your love for the Lord is evident and contagious. Again, our season was tough, but believe it was necessary and established by the Lord. I only pray the best for you because you deserve that.

I don't like that this had to be done over email, so if you want to talk about it more, that is fine. I totally understand.

I instantly felt a sense of freedom and ease as I pondered the thought after sending this cowardly email. It was as if a thousand-pound weight had been placed on my chest for the past eight months and was finally being lifted off. There was almost a skip in my step when I asked her to meet me by the beach to discuss the contents of my email and put an end to the relationship.

Happily Never Again

This was in no small way cowardly on my end. I'll never forget the moment I ended our relationship. We met at a park by the water. I had my sunglasses on, and she asked me to take them off. I was exposed. I was vulnerable. I told her I couldn't be with her, even after meeting her parents and discussing plans to one day propose. I knew this would crush her, but I also knew the relationship wasn't right. We left the park and never really spoke again outside of our roles as youth leaders.

Not only had I led her astray, but I'd essentially painted a target on my back — one perfect for Gordon's shooting practice. His mysterious "advice" had apparently reflected the strong feelings he had for Sarah but was too cowardly to tell me directly. As a result, his allegiance was to her, and I had become the enemy. From that moment on, I became embroiled in a battle to maintain my image in the church — a relentless quest that eventually led to my departure and liberation.

In need of profound damage control, I met with Ryan to explain how things happened between Sarah and me. But, again, he had punted me off to Gordon, so he was left in the dark (aka, the interpretations of Gordon and others). So, I sent him an email in follow up to our meeting since I felt he did not completely understand why I had ended things with Sarah:

Email: Me to Pastor Ryan
Date: July 3, 2011

Subject: Clear up any confusion...

Hey Pastor [Ryan],

I wanted to clarify a bit from my conversation with you yesterday and the text I sent you. I have been in a whirlwind of emotions and confusion these past couple days due to the situation with [Sarah] and me. In recognition of this turmoil, I have come to realize it has been a result of my unwillingness and fear of letting the Lord change my heart and perspective on the idea of [Sarah] and I potentially getting back together. With this, I have realized my running away from the idea in trying to validate my stance through reason and rationality. Your challenge to me yesterday had been exactly what the Lord was trying to speak to me: "Am I still called." With the potential calling back into this relationship, it must consist of a change of my heart and perspective. At first, the idea of the Lord changing my heart scared me much, but in recognition of it being THE LORD who would change my heart and perspective, it would ultimately be something I would want and desire. The text I sent you at 4:00pm was in recognition of that and being ok with the Lord doing this if it was His calling for us to be together.

I have typed up a detailed paragraph of my fears for this relationship continuing, and if you would like to see it, please let me know and I will send it to you. I originally put it in this email, but took it out because if it is not necessary, I wouldn't want you to be subject to it :)

I know the struggles I am currently dealing with as they have become evident in this relationship. My lack of understanding of love and tweaked version of it has become very prevalent through this relationship. I know the Lord is wanting to deal with me on this, and yes, I really do want Him to! I know the joy set before me in this is to love people unconditionally with the understanding of God's love for me and for others. The calling thus far consists of whether the Lord is calling me to experience this with [Sarah], or whether our season is over in terms of the Lord using this relationship to reveal this issue and have it thus be dealt with Him alone or another. I know, however, that reentering the relationship with [Sarah] would have to be a complete calling from the Lord and an understanding that the Lord has changed my heart and perspective on it. I don't see the character of the Lord to allow me to endure without me having a love for [Sarah] in this that validates her calling to this relationship. With that said, Lord, change my heart and perspective or continue to have us apart.

Thank you, Pastor [Ryan], for your unwavering stance in this and redirecting me to the Lord. I know this has been a challenge for you in dealing with me through this and I apologize for how hard it's been. I have shared A LOT with you, which has been hard for me to do. It has always been hard for me to trust others, especially from the past I have been delivered from. It has often been used against me, which only makes me shut people out in fears of being hurt again. I feel like I can trust you, which at times usually becomes a waterfall of everything going on for me. The Lord is teaching me how to not be such a pent-up & waterfall person, so I am sorry if I have been too much :) Thank you again Pastor [Ryan] and I can't even explain to you how much I am blessed to call you my pastor and to learn from you!

--

God Bless You!

Needless to say, the damage was done, and there was no turning back.

Shortly after moving to Los Angeles, I reached out to Sarah through Facebook Messenger, who had married the man she dated days after we broke up. I apologized to her for how I entered a relationship with her during a season in my life when I was in denial of my sexuality. I explained to her how I was now an openly gay man, living my truth for the first time. I wanted her to know that nothing about her made our union the shitshow it was, but my insecurity of embracing my homosexuality.

Her response was to block me.

HELPLESS & ... HUNGRY?

Ryan shielded me from Gordon's blows, but the damage from his shots seemed to leave permanent marks. Things were different between Ryan and me, and it was starting to become noticeable. There was tension in our meetings, which were now shorter and less intimate. His fuse was shorter with me, which in turn started to reveal the layers of deception in my mind. I persisted with caution, knowing from the experience of other members of this church that I could one day be sent to the guillotine for suspected treason should I test his authority.

Cracks in the Teapot

There were many cracks in the teapot. From what I remember, I never really felt truly secure in my faith. I constantly worried about how others could hear God (one housemate and many others claimed to listen to an audible voice) when sometimes all I heard were my thoughts telling me I was a fake. Nevertheless, I pressed on, hoping to one day hear the same voices others claimed to hear; I thought it was my fault that I hadn't heard them too. "I must not have enough faith," I concluded.

The most impactful incident that challenged my faith was the charge I took one Black Friday after sitting outside a Best Buy with some friends from Bayside. After their Thanksgiving meal, a group from church decided to pitch a spot in line for the early morning opening. As I arrived, I felt a sense of Christian duty to proselytize – it was a moment for me to shine in front of my peers.

Early on in my Christian journey, I learned that proselytizing separated Evangelical churches from most other denominations. It was the cornerstone and backbone of the entire belief system: without proselytizing, there would be no growth in the church. So I asked the group, "Why don't we go and evangelize to the other shoppers in line?" One family decided to go with me, while the others stayed to hold our spots.

We made our way down the line, hoping to find someone to receive our inquiry to speak to them about Jesus. Eventually, we came upon a group of kids who looked like they were in high school. I thought to myself, "Perfect!" Not only was I pastor of outreach, but at the time, I was also next in line to become the youth pastor. So I thought this was a great opportunity, especially since one of the girls with me was in our high school youth group.

It became quickly apparent that I had no idea what I was getting myself and the others into. We got our asses handed to us in plastic bags when they proved they knew the Bible better than any of us (and contradicted our claims with Bible verses). I dutifully tried to redirect the conversation. I took the classic notes from the book of Acts in the Bible where Paul made his testimony the most significant selling point to the gospel of Jesus.

It didn't occur to me that the group we were preaching to had witnessed our departure from our place in line as we made our pilgrimage to seek out lost souls. They artfully pointed out the hypocrisy of my message – how I preached that the love and compassion of Jesus were more important than worldly things. Yet, here we were, standing in line to beat out our fellow humans for the best-priced television. They dealt a final blow – a total knockout.

I picked my jaw up from the ground and walked back, but my head hung low, and I was shaking. Not only had these high schoolers schooled me in my own game, but they'd humiliated me in front of my peers. My identity as pastor of outreach felt compromised – I'd failed the test of evangelism. Here I was trying to be the "good pastor," yet I'd led my sheep into the hands of wolves. Upon our return to the group, I was too stunned to share what had taken place, so I pulled out a Christian cliché used in times like these: "They are clearly lost souls and can't see the truth, just as the Scriptures have said." We stood in a circle and prayed for them.

Little did I know that the one who was truly lost was me.

Through the years, my Christian life only amplified the desperation I experienced regularly. I began as a deeply insecure and wounded child seeking Christianity as a cure for my homosexual feelings. This morphed into a full-fledged lifestyle of denial and wishful thinking – that one day I would be straight and married with kids. This pursuit of the white, heterosexual Christian lifestyle was evident in my dating habits (or, more precisely, lack thereof). I believed in mind-altering explanations of my faith to push myself away from any reasonable argument against what I thought was the absolute truth.

I was convinced I had the cure to the world's pain and suffering. So I justified anything away that negated the message of the church. Lady Gaga, I once told the youth in my sermon, was possessed by the devil because she had exchanged her soul for fame and fortune. Ironically, Lady Gaga later became my role model in leaving the faith after watching a recording of her sharing how she started to say "no" to things she didn't want to do. Eventually, she said, she could look in the mirror and say, "Yes, I can go to bed with you every night because that person, I know that person. That person has balls, that person has integrity, that person has an opinion, that person doesn't say yes…". She talked about having an extreme amount of integrity in who you are, questioning why you are unhappy, and changing your life to make yourself happy. Her vulnerability, authenticity, and love for people were a roadmap for me to be a decent human being and recognize that I could care for people without religion.

Helpless to Homeless

As pastor of outreach, it was my duty to handle any matter of benevolence. While the role was about expanding the church base by preaching the gospel and inspiring converts, my favorite part was helping people. I genuinely believed the best help anyone could give another was leading them to Jesus (*before* taking care of their physical needs) — a belief regularly preached during church service.

We were constantly told that a person's physical needs weren't as important as the ultimate need for eternal life through the salvation of Jesus. This didn't prevent me from going out of my way to help someone, but it definitely set the tone and established my motive for *why*. All benevolence requests were meant to be a means to further the gospel of Jesus at this church; there was no other way to give.

This way of giving became the norm in my ministry, as we tried to find ways to enter the door to someone's heart to get them to accept Jesus. We constantly walked the streets looking for desperate souls. I even got us a booth at the local farmer's market on Saturdays to spread the good news about Jesus and our church. Then one day, volunteering became the turning point in my perspective.

At first, there was nothing out of the ordinary about this day. I left my morning job, headed to the church, and had just settled into my makeshift back office when I got a phone call from the front desk. The church secretary informed me that there was a gentleman seeking assistance. She didn't say much other than that he was in desperate need of help to pay his utility bills. I grasped the situation's sensitivity and immediately stopped what I was doing to head for the office.

As I approached, I saw a man sitting behind the counter; his head hung low. I could tell even from a distance that he was experiencing a string of unfortunate events and was in desperate need of help. When I came through the door, he sprang up from his seat to greet me. After niceties and small talk, I asked him how I could assist. His eyes welled up as he proceeded to tell me his story.

He and his wife had been evicted from their apartment and stayed in a hotel room, along with their kids. He'd lost his job and was unable to pay his utility bills, which seemed to be one of the sources of his eviction. He could really use some help — specifically, he wanted to know if the church could help him pay some of the utility bills he shamefully carried in his hands.

My heart sank. As much as I glossed over the façade of my faith, this situation seemed dire and struck at a significant heartstring. I felt deeply for this man. I've always felt for the down and out and can't help but think that my own story of being bullied was a formative experience. I expressed my condolences and felt deeply that this was something we could do but that I'd have to run it by the senior pastor. This wasn't unusual; it was the case for everything I did, primarily if it dealt with money.

When I knocked on Ryan's door, he told me to come in. He looked up from his church-purchased iPad, asking how he could help. The iPad, a seemingly insignificant detail at the moment, seemed somehow magnified after hearing about the man's situation. I told Ryan the story of the man's desperation and humiliation and how I really wanted to help the guy out.

Ryan was skeptical (a trait not foreign to him regarding the needy). "We don't know the truth about his condition; who's to say it wasn't of his own making?" I was shocked but also somehow not surprised. There were plenty of lessons in this church about "reaping what you sow," but for me, this felt different and personal. After all, there were kids involved.

I couldn't imagine what it would be like to be a child and have your whole world ripped out from under you. I also couldn't imagine what this man was feeling — being the provider for his family and failing to the point where he was begging for money. I was baffled by Ryan's response but shied away from challenging his wisdom on the matter.

He informed me that even if we wanted to do this, we couldn't because we'd already blown through the outreach budget. This was surprising; it was news to me that we even had funding for outreach. I constantly footed the bills on purchases for my ministry, thinking this was my way of giving the church. He said it was $300 a month (apparently, my proposed salary had become the budget). He instructed me to let the man know we'd love to help, but since we didn't have the financial resources to do so, we could provide him with donated food from the pantry. "Oh, and don't forget to tell him about Jesus — the thing he and his family need most in their lives, especially in this time."

That last request hit me differently; it stung and struck me as both cold and insincere for the first time. This wasn't even close to what Jesus would have done, I thought. I couldn't imagine the contrast between what Jesus would have done in this situation and how we were responding. There was hypocrisy in our actions that became apparent to me for the first time. I later pondered things like: How can the church afford a $1,000 handheld computer for Ryan's sermons and not $50 to help a family get back on its feet? The glow on Ryan's face from the iPad became a metaphor for the light that was starting to grow inside me, revealing the truth about this church. I was beginning to wake up and was disgusted.

As hard as it was to have the church control my every move, these were the moments that chipped away at my soul. They became painfully frequent as I started to awaken from my slumber. In the beginning, I was too insecure and cowardly to address my concerns and let moments like these slip through the cracks. I believed the roles each of the leaders possessed were ordained by God, so to challenge them was to challenge God. But this event couldn't have been more revealing of the nature of this church's leadership style. If I were to have any part in this, I'd have to compromise my deepest convictions on what the Bible actually called Christians to do for those in need. I recalled Jesus' many calls to take care of the widows and orphans and the unrelenting love Jesus had for children and the down and out.

I knew I was never going to let this happen again.

Gaining My Stride

The more I asserted myself, the more pushback I got. The process always started and ended with Ryan: complaints from other congregants were submitted to him, and he found time in our weekly sessions to make me aware of the concerns. Often he agreed with the complaint, and sometimes he didn't, but they were nonetheless relayed to me to "pray over." I was asked to consider the concern and not "overact" or "overanalyze;" just receive the feedback and make adjustments accordingly.

The complaints seemed endless. They covered everything from what I posted on social media to what I wore; it appeared there was some impossible standard I constantly failed to meet. This chipped away at what little identity I had in my position at the church. I became paranoid by the bickering and backstabbing. I wasn't sure who to trust anymore and was cautious about sharing anything. I felt like I was on a deserted island, being attacked left and right.

I was mad at myself for having shared my stories with Gordon and wondered whether my romance with Jake or relationship with Sarah had made things worse for me. I wondered whether the prayers I gave before the prayer team members were perceived as concerning since some comments by Ryan were about my doctrinal soundness. No matter where I went or who I was with, information always seemed to find its way to Ryan's desk, and he'd always address it with me. It was clear there were eyes on me at all times.

I felt tense when certain people were in the room, especially since I knew about their cunningness — they pretended to be my friend to my face but painted me as questionable to others. I was not in a good place by the time shit really hit the fan — a fact apparent to many. Then a moment of weakness left the scent of blood in the water; just like those of the past, my day of judgment was on the horizon. It became clear that my time had come to be nailed to the cross.

THOUGHT: ISOLATION & TRAUMA

"The intensely painful feeling or experience of believing that we are flawed and therefore unworthy of love and belonging. 'I am bad.' 'I am a mess.' The focus is on self, not behavior, with the result that we feel alone. Shame is never known to lead us toward positive change"

– Brene Brown.

Isolation is the Enemy

There is nothing more erosive to the soul than isolation. Feeling like you are the only one experiencing challenging situations or traumatic incidents. The world knowing of our secret crevices would be dreadful. In an attempt to protect our secrets, we bury them deep within ourselves. We find coping mechanisms that distract from the truth. Buried deep, depression and anxiety can begin to control our lives while shame becomes the captain of our ship.

Shame was the most powerful force that drew me to the church. The shame of my sexuality caused me to bury deep the parts of myself I found most frightening. As I grew deeper in the faith, I became more paranoid by the thought of others finding out that I was a fraud.

"What if they knew who I truly was?"

"Would I be ostracized from this community if they knew the thoughts that go through my head?"

Shame for what the church termed my "old nature" only festered within me as I continued in the faith. The fear of being exposed caused me to stuff my deepest secrets, which made me more isolated on an impoverished island.

The reality of isolation set in. I recall being in a group of people, yet I felt like I was all alone. The façade of the moment would eat away at my soul as I found it a laborious endeavor to keep up the expectations of who others desired me to be. I knew I couldn't indeed be myself for fear of being labeled a homosexual. So, the act continued, finding no rest for the weary as I *"pressed on toward the goal to win the prize for which God has called me."* I truly believed my oppression was my calling, even if it meant that I had to be isolated from everyone I knew.

Trauma

After leaving the faith, the results of my handlers became prevalent. Trauma, as defined by the American Psychological Association is:

> "an emotional response to a terrible event like an accident, rape or natural disaster. Immediately after the event, shock and denial are typical. Longer-term reactions include unpredictable emotions, flashbacks, strained relationships, and even physical symptoms like headaches or nausea. While these feelings are normal, some people have difficulty moving on with their lives."

There were plenty of examples of situations that created my trauma in the church. Most destructive was the doctrine that supported the actions of my abusers - the doctrine of salvation. Being told that I was a "dirty rotten sinner," that I was "destined for eternal damnation unless the intervention of an 'all-loving' God" became the motive behind the abuse. Keeping me in isolation from my secular friends and family was a tactic deployed to keep me dependent upon the system of control. Being released to the "real world" brought light to the traumas of my past, exposing the deep-seated beliefs of self-loathing.

My body began to show the signs. Gastrointestinal issues and the like manifested as they revealed the tight grip I held on to for fear of being exposed. I put on a mask to hide the pain, resorting to stimulants to ease the tension. My physical issues became so excruciating that I had to seek out medical attention. Every doctor told me I was healthy, and it could only be a form of emotional duress. It was the first time I was introduced to the concept of our bodies keeping score – tied behind each ailment was a story and warning my body was trying to tell me - trauma.

The fear of not being myself became more potent than the fear of exposing myself as I slowly became curious about my identity. Being tucked away in my first studio apartment in Los Angeles (a less than 300 square foot box), it was clear that there were too many holes in the argument to continue in my life of celibacy and isolation. The habits built by my former life of lies were revealing themselves more self-destructive than helpful. What was once the ultimate calling for "the way to live" by the church now became clear was my ultimate oppressor.

Throughout building my new community, I am learning how to trust others as I learn how to trust myself. Not only does my old belief system no longer serve me, but it was becoming a burden too heavy to bear.

As I pressed in deeper into holistic healing, it became apparent that my former life of oppression and isolation was the ultimate root of my body's manifestations. I had placed my identity in the hands of others, not trusting what my body was trying to communicate to me. I allowed my handlers to push me deeper into isolation with every form of control through rules and punishment. I felt shame for who I was, and at times regretted life itself. I needed to learn to trust my initial instincts; a process started when I ultimately decided to leave Bayside Church.

LIBERTY

Over nine months, attacks on my identity worsened. What were once subtle complaints and requests to be prayed about, I was now ordered to make hard changes to my behavior.

The attacks began when it got out that I was listening to podcast teachings from Pastor Joe, my former pastor at Real Life Church. He'd made a name for himself in the Christian community for his in-depth, surfer-style teachings. I was longing for community and a new perspective after losing allies due to my perceived failures. Unfortunately, lines in the sand were being drawn, and I could feel the tensions between people I loved, knowing they too had to decide whether to align with the leadership at Bayside or me. Often they were on the side of the church, and the island of isolation I found myself on became ever more desolate.

The podcasts from Real Life gave me a sense of refuge and made me homesick. I couldn't help but make trips back home to go to church and see my old friends. As awkward as the reunions were, it was nice to feel some nostalgia for the good old days when I was in high school. I saw some of my former Christian friends, then grown up with families of their own. Just seeing them brought a sense of family even though we hardly knew anything about each other anymore. It was a glimmer of hope in a time of darkness.

"Traitor!" - Anonymous

Starving for a new perspective, I listened to as many different church podcasts as I could get my hands on. Filled with nostalgia and wonder, I realized the world I'd created was much smaller than the world around me. So I constantly posted on social media about the different sources of media I was partaking in, hoping it would be a blessing to others.

After I posted about one of the podcasts from Real Life Church, one of the prayer leaders of the missionary group I oversaw at the time raised this as a matter of concern.

She "anonymously" brought up to Ryan the fact that I was listening to this questionable pastor, as well as other well-known Calvinists. Since the beliefs of Bayside were grounded in the Arminian doctrine, Calvinism was a blasphemous doctrinal belief and needed to be corrected (Calvinists believe in predestination, whereas Arminians believe that anyone can be saved, as long as you confess Jesus as Lord. Stupid semantics, I know).

One night before Wednesday service, I was pulled into Ryan's office. While neatly avoiding the source of the hysteria concerning the podcast, Ryan told me someone in the church was concerned about my doctrinal beliefs due to a post on Facebook of a Bible verse that supported the Calvinist doctrine. Rather than address the podcast directly, he found a way to call attention to the subject by merely referring to a Bible verse commonly used to support the doctrine of predestination.

Yes, you read that right. It was simply a Bible verse that he took issue with — with no commentary whatsoever. Shocked and shaken, I had no idea what to make of this as I tried to discern who had the problem to approach them and explain why I'd posted that specific verse. Ryan told me this person desired to remain anonymous but was an influential church member. *Coward*, I thought. I had a sense of who it was and asked whether it was indeed the person I was thinking about; Ryan nodded yes.

I consented to his request to take down my post, and Ryan said he'd issue an apology on my behalf.

Later that night, after reflecting on how this had gone down, I texted Ryan to reassure him that I was not promoting the Calvinist doctrine — that I was simply posting a verse that had struck me in my morning devotional. I was scared this would be the end of my ministry, that I'd be asked to resign considering my perceived confrontational theological beliefs. Fortunately, my responses seemed to smooth things over...until the next shoe dropped.

Cult of Personality

The fact is, targeting my Facebook post wasn't effective - I think Ryan thought I could read between the lines and grasp that his concern was more about me listening to Pastor Joe and his Calvinist-soaked sermons than the Bible verse. But I hadn't understood that and continued to listen to these podcasts, clutching on to them even more tightly as I felt the ground under me crack and crumble.

The next time was the final time on the subject. Once again, I found myself in Ryan's office, this time to discuss a post of mine about a specific sermon. I'd found it very beneficial and thought others would appreciate it, as well. Ryan, however, expressed his concern for my Calvinist tenancies and decided to be more direct. He said he'd noticed I was listening to Pastor Joe and told me he'd done some research on him and had concerns about his image. Not only was he concerned about his doctrinal beliefs, but he also feared I was following someone who was a narcissist. He said he thought Joe was someone who loved the spotlight — "cult of personality" was his specific diagnosis.

Ryan also said he was concerned that my belief system would be corrupted by listening to him and would eventually contrast with the doctrinal beliefs of the church I was serving. He ended this conversation by giving me a grave warning, encouraging me to stop listening to the podcasts. I left feeling both indignant and betrayed, my head hung low and contemplating my next steps.

This was the first incident where I mustered up the confidence to push back against his judgmental claims. I felt protective of my former pastor and thought Ryan wasn't fair in his judgment, especially since he'd never met him. So, I wrote him an email saying I understood his concern but that I also felt guilty about our conversation and judgment of Joe — claiming part of the blame in hopes to soften the blow:

Date: November 21, 2011
Subject: Reflections of our conversation...

Hey Pastor [Ryan]!

I was reflecting on our conversation on [Pastor Joe] on Friday and I wanted to express some viewpoints I did not share due to my fear of offending (I'm telling you; the Lord is really working on me in regard to people-pleasing). I did some research on Cult of Personality and I do not believe at all that this is descriptive of [him]. I recall listening to a message recently on why they are doing live broadcasts, and what I got from it was [Real Life Church pastor] heart-checking himself and confessing his weakness in popularity. He said that the Lord made it very clear through many incidents and through others that this was what they were called to do.

Although I mentioned I did not agree with it, I confess after examining the situation, I cannot say here nor there if I agree with their live broadcasting but know and trust that this is what the Lord called them to. As I mentioned in his recent sermons, they have been the complete opposite of self-promotion. I have heard a humility and honesty like no other in a pastor in his recent messages. After looking at his Facebook as well, I noticed that it was no different from other pastors (the glorifying pictures are those taken by other people and professional photographers in whom I was personal friends with. They were just taking pictures of the events and tagged [him] in them). This is NOT a defense of [Real Life Church], but a realization and confession of assumptions and perspectives on

> our parts not being accurate. I trust the Lord's calling on his life just as I do yours and know that he is a sinner just like us.
>
> I really appreciate your concern for me in not being swayed by man and finding my identity in Christ alone. I have recognized your intent of leading in the Lord's ways as you are called to as my pastor and am truly grateful for your concern. I want to let you know that the season I am in has been a really challenging but fruitful one and the Lord is currently using messages & books by [Real Life Church] and others to refine me through this. Thank you again for your pastoring and am blessed to be entrusted to your leadership as Christ leads you!

I thought it would go over better if I assumed some responsibility for misjudging, as well. So I told Ryan I disagreed with his characterization of Joe and that I needed to express what I had feared saying during our conversation. I received no response, nor was it ever addressed again.

This was yet another drop in the bucket.

A Steady Trickle

After the debacle of the Facebook Bible verse and podcast posts, I decided to leave out commentary on my posts

- I just included Bible verses to test the nature of my monitoring and subsequent requests to take them down. I don't remember how often this happened, but it got to the point where I could count down the minutes from posting to receiving a text or call from Ryan asking me to take down a post or question why I'd posted something. It was as if the Bible itself was a direct threat to the church, which in hindsight doesn't sound all too far from the truth.

They also sought to control where I went during my free time. The rules of Bayside's former senior pastor regarding alcohol were still in effect and on steroids. It got to the point where I was no longer allowed to go country line dancing since there was a bar at the venue, and it wouldn't look good for me to be seen there. I could barely go to restaurants without wondering whether it was OK for me to be there. Birthday parties for my few secular friends were shunned unless confirmed that there would be no alcohol present.

It wasn't just the presence of alcohol that prevented me from going to places I wanted. I was experiencing a lull in my relationships. I'd been harshly judged for my breakup with Sarah, so it felt strange to try to maintain friendships with the people my age at church. They'd seemed to form alliances with her and kept me at arm's length.

I looked up the neighboring town's college church group and asked Ryan's permission to visit their weekly services.

Rather than be supportive, he was shocked by my request, wondering why I wasn't finding fellowship in our church. I expressed my grievances, pointing out that our church's median age was much older than mine. Even considering this, I was asked not to go out of fear that I'd be recruited to join their church. This was yet another heavy blow for me, as I became even more isolated.

Lost in Translation

I didn't relate to anyone at church anymore. As time went on, I became the odd man out. Before, I'd been in the inner circle, talking about other Christians and how they were doing things wrong according to our interpretation of the Bible. We'd discussed how our way was the "only way." But now, I was the one receiving criticism, and it didn't feel great. I finally understood what it meant to be in a community where you're looking in from the outside.

Once, after walking into the office, I heard Ryan having an open conversation with the rest of the staff. I could hear them laughing as they discussed the different translations of the Bible and how the New King James Version (NKJV) was the only authoritative translation (due to original manuscripts from which it was sourced). Ryan continued by talking about the other translations, even questioning the faith of those who used specific translations.

His argument was the following: How could they really understand the weight of the gospel if they were reading a translation that didn't interpret the scriptures correctly? This was disgusting, and I left the room wondering how that kind of conversation could even be entertained. It made sense to me that they didn't think Catholics were going to heaven since they worshiped saints (who were believed to be idols) — but questioning the faith of other Evangelicals was going too far for me. I thought about the people I loved most, who read different translations of the Bible. I wondered whether, if they met these people, they'd genuinely believe they were destined to hell simply because they read a different translation of the Bible?

More drops in the bucket.

Opening the Floodgates

In the end, it wasn't their requirement that I install software to track my internet search history (on my private laptop) and report it to Ryan, nor the issues with my controversial choice of music (anything outside of Christian pop — like Taylor Swift — was frowned upon. God forbid they find out I loved Lady Gaga. Also, yes, they had an issue with me listening to Taylor Swift's breakup songs. It apparently gave the youth a dangerous impression of secular love). It wasn't even being pimped out like some sort of Christian bachelor to hide the possibility that I was some homosexual pervert with a secret lover somewhere. All those things were palatable to me.

The straw that finally broke the camel's back related to my education.

To this day, I love school. Learning new things piqued my interest, and even as a devout Christian, I found science-related subjects fascinating — I put my Christian spin on evolution and creationism. However, after receiving three associate degrees and derailing my professional career aspirations by attending this church's Bible college, I became more interested in pursuing an accredited degree.

Although Bible college was what I'd wanted concerning learning biblical knowledge, it lacked my desired credentials. The Bible college was a satellite school to the home church in Southern California and wasn't accredited. This meant the bachelor's degree I'd receive from it wasn't recognized as a credible degree, and I'd have issues applying for master's programs in the future. So, after attending this Bible college for over three years, I felt the need to do some research on how to get an accredited bachelor's degree.

I knew I needed to run this by Ryan. I could tell he wasn't thrilled by the idea, but he could sense the desperation in my tone. He controlled many different aspects of my life and knew I'd come to a breaking point one day. He nor I didn't realize it at the time, but my education was nonnegotiable. After expressing my desires, we agreed that I'd continue to get my bachelor's degree in biblical studies from an accredited institution. I had to get approval from him about which school I'd attend before applying. This seemed like a reasonable compromise at the time, and I immediately began my search.

I spent months deliberating. Some schools were an absolute no — they either didn't align with the church's doctrinal belief or were too liberal (the main complaint). Finally, after exhaustive research, only one school met all his requirements: Liberty University. There was no way he could disagree with this choice. They were doctrinally sound and reputable in the Evangelical community. They would give me the freedom to do all my courses online so I wouldn't have to move away and forsake my pastoral roles.

After discussing this with him, I thought I'd picked a winner. Then, shortly after our conversation, he sent me an email expressing his concerns about aligning myself with Liberty University and Jerry Falwell. I was finishing up work when I got the email, already exhausted when I saw the subject line.

As I started to read it, deep-seated anger welled up within me. My face turned red, and my fists clenched. I wanted to throw my phone across the parking lot. I'd had enough. I was fuming:

Email: [Ryan] to me
Date: June 27, 2012
Subject: Liberty University and Jerry Farwell

Hey bro,

I was doing some homework on Liberty University and came across some concerning info to take to prayer.

Just to let you know that Liberty University was founded by Jerry Falwell, please do you homework on this guy. The school is being ran by his son.

There is A LOT of controversy surrounding him, and as a graduate you will, like it or not, represent him and or his ministries, just as a [Bayside Bible college] graduate will represent [mother church]/and our [mother church pastor].

I would agree with everything on their Doctrine statement, but Jerry Falwell is know for being a televangelist, money seeking, good ol' boy.

I just want you to be prepared and know what you're getting into. Give me a call if you want to talk more. Don't

---

> read more into this, or think I'm wiggin out. Just trying to look out for you!
>
> with all love and respect
>
> *Links to Wikipedia and YouTube

I can't remember whether I called the church office or texted him, but I know I said: "15 minutes, your office."

My bucket runneth over.

Coming to an End

As I drove to the church, I got angrier and angrier. My years of devotion and sacrifice replayed in my mind. I recalled everything I'd given up on becoming a pastor. I remembered all the times I'd chosen the church over my satisfaction, knowing that one day all my sacrifices would pay off. I woke up entirely to the manipulation and control tactics they'd used upon me and became angry at myself for willingly accepting it. I thought about my family — how I'd isolated myself from them. I found myself hoping they'd one day forgive me. This was it — I was no longer going to take it. I scripted in my mind what I'd say, not knowing how this would play out.

I pulled into the church parking lot, took a deep breath, and stormed into the office. Ryan was waiting for me, a look of confusion and curiosity on his face. I entered his office, closed the door, and let the torrent flow. I could feel my body shake as I let out my frustration and anger. For the first time, I determined what I wanted, what I needed, and how I wasn't getting any of it from the church. It was a clarity of mind like no other in my life. I talked about how he claimed to care for me, that he had my best interests in mind, but little did he know I'd been looking at gay porn on and off for the past four years.

I told him that if he had any inkling of care for me, he would have known about this and many other secrets I'd been keeping from him. That was just the tip of the iceberg as I laid out all the grievances I had and how I'd become increasingly more guarded and paranoid due to his actions. He was utterly speechless, tears forming in his eyes. I didn't care; it was finally my turn to let him know how I felt.

His only words had to do with his shock and shame for it coming to this. He then asked, "When would you like your last day to be?" I told him, "Ideally, this Sunday." The last thing I remember him saying was, "*No matter where you are or what you do, God is going to use you in miraculous ways for His glory.*" The words fell on deaf ears at the time since his actions were much more powerful.

I can't explain the heavy burden lifted from me as I walked out of his office. The other staff members looked at me, wondering what the hell had just happened. For the first time, I didn't care, and I knew I was free.

Ryan requested that I draft a message to the youth group and submit it for approval before Sunday (so as not to have a rogue message). I understood his desire for damage control and obliged — this was the last request I would ever respond to. It was one of the most challenging messages I had to give since I loved those kids to no end. I knew it would be hard and that nothing could have prepared me for it. I did go a bit rogue in that I expressed my absolute admiration for them and heartbreak in leaving.

Then I went home, finished packing up my things, gave my two weeks' notice at work, and let my family know I was moving back home to figure out my life. I was finally free — I had been liberated.

PART

5

RESURRECTION

ALLER SANS RETOUR

In the early fall of 2012, I left Bayside Church. I sat in the twin-sized bed of my childhood, staring at my stuff piled in boxes around me. I felt a sense of both renewal and fear. I was embarking upon a new chapter and worried about the path before me. The canvas screamed white; I could start the stroke of the brush anywhere.

My sister and I shared the same room that my brother and I had once shared as children. My sister was also rebounding from an alternate life. She had moved to a different area to be with her boyfriend, and when that relationship ended, my dad and I had helped her move back home. Both young adults, we were back in the same town again, living in the same space. We shared a sense of aimlessness mixed with cautious anticipation for what was to come. This experience allowed us to bond on a deeper level as it seemed we'd both hit rock bottom at the same time.

One of my favorite memories with her from this time was a night when we sat on the pier, sharing a bottle of Menage A Trois wine and reminiscing about the good old days. This was my first taste of alcohol since leaving the church, and it felt good to get buzzed without getting drunk. We listened to music, laughed, and cried a bit. To this day, we talk about that night with a sense of fondness. There was a sense of camaraderie and familiarity that had been missing since I'd entered the depths of Bayside Church.

After about a month, we were leaving a coffee shop where we'd been studying when my sister got into my truck. Before I put the key in the ignition, she said, "I need to tell you something." I paused, wondering what she wanted to say. She proceeded to tell me how she and my brother had hated being around me when I was involved at Bayside — how they'd avoided interacting with me at any cost. I'd been a judgmental, arrogant, insufferable asshole. She said she saw a change in me now, that I was different ... and that she'd missed this version of me. It was true; I had become less rigid about my faith and more accepting of the people in my life.

Reenlisting

My faith hadn't entirely left me as I quickly submerged myself back into Real Life Church – the church of my youth. Although being there was familiar from my high school days and the times I'd visited over the years, joining again was like starting over. The friends I'd known in school had either moved away or had families that kept them busy. So I did what I knew best: enrolled in Bible study groups and volunteered to build community.

I soon reached out to Real Life's senior pastor, Pastor Joe, who I was sure would remember me. As soon as I walked through the church doors, my defenses dropped. I was greeted by the vast wingspan of Pastor Joe's intimate embrace. A towering figure, I felt like I was consumed by a tidal wave of love and concern. Curious about my past and shocked by my return, he probed me with questions. After running through a brief history, Joe felt it was best to connect me with Pastor Todd, who recalled me from Bible studies he had led when I was in high school.

Todd was the opposite of Joe. He was a methodical, analytical character. Head of the church finances, he always was a step ahead of everyone. Kind-hearted and socially awkward, I found his personality strangely comforting as I was not intimidated by his stature. In addition, he wasn't troubled by my past because we had built a foundation in my high school days.

Todd and I met up for coffee, and I began telling him my story – how I'd been attending Bayside Church, a church in a small community up north for the past several years, and how I had worked my way up to becoming the outreach pastor. I mentioned the fallout and resentment I still carried towards Pastor Ryan. I also talked about this deep anger I felt, which I now know was a projection of all the guilt and shame I felt at being duped by the people involved at Bayside. I wondered how I could have been so stupid as to let it get as far as it did.

Todd assured me my anger was understandable but not necessary. He said that I simply "needed to pray to forgive those who hurt you, regardless of whether they ever talked to you again." He recommended I at least reach out to Ryan to make amends. I drafted an email that Todd reviewed, and I sent it off! I felt like it was a new beginning by putting my past behind me, and I was finally restarting my life.

However, something felt different. What was different this time was that I did it with less zeal and more skepticism. The steady trickle of my departure from my Christian life began to take hold.

Last Love

I met Scarlett at one of the Bible study group meetings. She was a vibrant personality with a knack for authenticity. She wasn't like the other girls at church – she paved her own way in life, not becoming brainwashed by the expectations of a single woman in the church. It wasn't that she wasn't interested in dating, but her strong independence made her quite the struggle to tame for even the most secure male in the church.

She constantly brought substance and depth to the Bible study group, challenging the status quo. It was what attracted me to her most – her fiery zeal for genuine conversation and dismantling the patriarchy. She worked as the tasting room manager at a local winery, which defiled the norms of my former life at Bayside – working in sin.

We hit it off one night as she once said to me, "you know, you are like a prince in an ivory tower." She caught me off guard – how did she see my façade so blatantly? Never had anyone called me out so abruptly and with such accuracy! I was used to people fawning over my charisma, but this girl saw right through me. She knew that my charm and charisma was most often a front – only giving enough information & care to keep people at a comfortable distance.

Scarlett was quite literally the girl next door; she lived with a group of girls in an apartment next to my parents' house. I now found it more of a pleasure to visit my parents, hoping to catch her at home to chat it up. I knew this girl was special, and I wanted to learn more about her. As we started to hang out more, I began to see the spicy mommy in her, naming her "Kristen Wiig" on my phone and me "Playboy All Day" in hers (still holding firm to this day). We had a kindred spirit that got tangled in the wires of my interpretation of our relationship.

As I started to court her, she could sense my shyness when asking if she wanted to grab a drink alone sometime. She played along but quickly set the ground rules – if I was going to pursue her, I best be committed, or she would add me to the list of notches in her book of conquests. I took heed to her words but thought nothing of it – if she was to be a bride, there were clear guidelines that the Bible had for women. Although I was coming to a more liberal interpretation of the Bible in my theological beliefs, my quest to find a submissive wife was hard to overcome. The rigidity of my attempts left me bare before her.

After a series of frustrating conversations, we decided to meet up for coffee to determine the trajectory of our relationship. I knew in my heart of hearts that if it weren't going to work out with this woman, it would never work with any woman. After kicking my ass in a lesson of authenticity, I realized that my rigidity in my ideals of a companion was suppressive and controlling. She let me know how I made her feel and questioned if we could have a friendship after this was all said and done. Swallowing my pride for fear of losing her, I apologized for how I was acting, admitting to her my struggles with homosexuality. This came as a surprise to her and changed the trajectory of our relationship. Scarlett became the last woman I would ever "love" (she once joked with one of my boyfriends that she was the last woman I ever loved and that I loved her first).

Thankfully, the awkwardness of our attempted love relationship blossomed into a dear friendship. To this day, I am happy to say that she has become one of few Christians for whom I have great depth and admiration.

New Beginnings

I committed to attending Liberty University after leaving Bayside, and it felt like another act of rebellion. I enrolled as a biblical studies major, pursuing my bachelor's degree as I tried to transfer courses from my former Bible college. Since that institution wasn't accredited, I had to start from scratch.

But after a year of the biblical studies program at Liberty University, I was itching for something different. I remembered my initial desire to go into accounting and kept that bookmarked in my mind. Then, after getting a failing grade on a paper in one of my Bible classes, I became acutely aware of the hypocrisy of Christianity. The essay was about deacons in the church and if there was biblical justification for women's roles to be filled. After a thoughtfully re-searched paper with Bible verses, theological references, and the like, my conclusion was that, indeed, women could be deacons. But unfortunately, the teacher failed me on the premise that it didn't align with the doctrinal beliefs of Lib-erty University. The doctrinal belief of this institution was that women were not allowed to serve as deacons in the church.

I thought, "what bullshit!" and pondered the ramifica-tions of these doctrinal differences. I realized that if I could have sound biblical references as to why women could be deacons, yet be faced with entirely contradictory beliefs with firm biblical references to justify the opposite, any-thing, and everything in the Bible was up to interpretation – based on the premise of the doctrinal beliefs adopted by each denomination. For example, Baptists believe you need to be physically baptized to get into heaven, while Evan-gelicals see it as a metaphor. Who's right? If one is wrong, then an entire denomination is destined for unjust eternal damnation.

Soon after this, I changed my major to accounting, and never looked back. This became the signature event that started the unraveling of my faith.

Real Christians

My last two years in the church were the best they could have been. I moved in with a group of guys from Real Life Church with whom I formed significant and substantial relationships (don't worry, no sexual explorations with any of these men this time), but I knew my faith was on shaky ground. Nevertheless, I was thankful to meet one of my best friends in this house, who to this day remains one of three Christian people who I've kept in my life – Scarlett, Emma, and Liam.

Liam was a caring, compassionate, and quiet man who lived his faith like none I had experienced. His love for people and God to this day makes me wonder why more Christians aren't like this man and his beautiful wife, Emma. He didn't lord his faith over anyone, as he desired to see the friends in his life flourish in all that they did. This was a breath of fresh air and gave me the freedom to explore my thoughts on problematic beliefs in the church that were never really challenged, as they were just chalked up as absolute truths. His example became my roadmap.

One of the issues I struggled with most hit close to home and was the essence of my identity crisis. My homosexual feelings were constantly there, but this time they felt right. I wrestled with this, digging deep into sermons and commentaries on the verses that talked about homosexuality.

When I was able to do this research on my own, I concluded that the hard stance in the church against homosexuality was also a crock of bullshit — that the church used it to keep them complacent. For an institution with such strong beliefs about homosexuality, the evidence didn't even come close to being either rational or reasonable. Slowly but surely, the mask began to fall as I became freer to express myself with this group of guys.

Shortly after moving in, our pad quickly became known as "The Haven." This name gained traction as our house became most known for the freedom people felt to be themselves within our four walls. We knew we were the outcasts of the church; the cliques of Real Life were more than evident. When we were infrequently invited to join the cool kids at events at their house (and trust me, they were infrequent), we would be filled with angst to leave so we could find solace in the authenticity we found in each other. So, we decided to have a home where anyone and everyone was invited and accepted, following the Christian motto of "come as you are." My siblings even found rest in this place – seamlessly making friends with Christian people who were normal and accessible.

My time at The Haven was greatly impressed by the friendship of two women who decided to make their visits more frequent. After coming home from work, I would be pleasantly greeted by their presence. We joked that they were like stray cats who we fed too much, but in reality, they felt like home. We even made sure to leave the back door unlocked if one of them stopped by unannounced and nobody was home to let them in. There was freedom in this house for men and women to be themselves and stay as late as they wanted with whoever was home (unlike the legalism at Bayside). We discussed life honestly and genuinely – expressing our deepest struggles and finding humor in everything. We also found time to make fun with each other; our playfulness became so much that we had to create a safe word for when we were actually serious: *panda* (a name I assigned to the adopted household cat who became mine when I left).

One of the women who impacted me the most was Emma. She was as real as anyone could get. She didn't hide behind a façade of perfection; instead, she constantly exposed her deepest insecurities and vulnerabilities. Emma became the pinnacle of my admiration as she demonstrated what strength looked like in weakness. She had her fair share of fake bullshit in life and looked for something much more substantial and intimate in her relationships. Her relationship with her God was a genuine pursuit and struggle that she demonstrated in every avenue of her life. Her kindness, vulnerability, and sarcasm brought me closer to experiencing the love of Jesus more than anyone has ever. She showed me what community and family truly meant.

It made sense when Emma and Liam became lovers. The news overjoyed me as we set out on a road trip to celebrate! We found ourselves in constant states of laughter and deep conversations as we set out to explore central California and the west coast. This road trip became such a turning point in my life as I was losing hope for all Christians. These two showed their power and strength in their individuality and authenticity, and compassion in their union. They were simply the perfect couple as they both shared in their imperfections. These two influential people have been the clearest examples of Christianity to this day. I am beyond honored to call these two my dearest friends still.

If only more Christians were more like them.

Embracing Change

Shortly after moving home, I set out to find a job. First, I reached out to a local recruiting firm, which placed me in a dispatch position within a local university's facilities department. I quickly made moves there, connecting with those in the accounting department. Eventually, I discovered that one of the financial officers needed a financial assistant, so I applied and was offered the position. After a year, I applied for a job in the accounting department and leveraged that to network with the accounting association club on campus.

If there was anything I was good at, it was using my charisma to expand my network. It was a trait that had brought me success as the outreach pastor. In addition, people were drawn to my joyful demeanor, not knowing it was also a front to keep people at bay. I didn't realize this was a coping mechanism until therapy, where I learned a healthier approach to letting people close in my life.

After successful interviews with several highly reputable accounting firms, I was offered a position in the Los Angeles office of the top accounting firm in the world. The fruits of my labor paid off as I set out to start a new life in the second-largest city in the United States. Moreover, the offer came at the perfect time; I knew this opportunity would allow me to explore my sexuality due to the city's reputation.

Finally Coming Out

My devotion to the faith continued to unravel as I started to explore my sexuality. Doing my research about homosexuality in the Bible brought me to the conclusion that what the church built its foundation on to justify its condemnation of the gay community was on shaky ground. Exercising my extensive Biblical knowledge, I concluded that the substance of the church's interpretation failed miserably to put into context the cultural climate each writer was explicitly writing to (not to mention that the word "homosexual" was interpreted from the word "sodomy" in the 20th century). Nevertheless, I was building the confidence within myself to come out of the closet eventually.

It was a no-brainer coming out of the closet for the first time to my cousin. Still, I was nervous as this was uncharted territory. Before ever thinking of owning my sexuality, I always prefaced my story about my homosexuality in the context of it being a detestable sin that God would heal. This time I was willing to stick my head out of my shell to embrace it, even though I felt like a rudderless ship. I contemplated talking to my siblings first but hesitated, knowing they had ridden the roller coaster of my disdain for homosexuality for so many years. Coming out to them may have been too much of a shock, I thought, so I knew that the best choice was coming out to my cousin. She always felt like a sister to me. We constantly joked that one of our fathers must've had an affair with one of our mothers and were separated at birth. It was the only explanation for how we ended up so much alike.

Mustering up the courage, I sent her a text telling her that I wanted to talk to her about something. Piquing her interest in my cryptic text, she told me to give her a call. I was shaking as I heard the telephone ring. It was as if I was riding a 7.2 magnitude earthquake, trying to keep my grip on my phone. I told her that I was going on a date, but it was not with a woman this time. Instead, I told her how I met a man in Europe on a dating app, and I would meet up with him there.

My tensions subsided as the news overjoyed her! Her love and compassion at that moment were nothing but genuine. She celebrated with me on this new endeavor and made me swear I would keep her posted along the way. Her tone put me at ease as I explored what it meant to be an openly gay man for the first time. I can still remember the pain from the smile on my face – beaming ear to ear with excitement and love. My cousin couldn't have been more graceful or supportive. To this day, we have one of the most genuine, authentic relationships. There are plenty of inside jokes between us – one being that we try to find our "in the closet time" at family gatherings to get away with a bottle of wine and talk about the men in my life.

European Romance

After coming out to my cousin, I booked my trip to Europe — a journey that would take place before I started my new job in LA. I told my housemates I'd be moving, and they set to work finding my replacement. Then I sold my truck, got a storage unit, and set out on my first European trip.

I was filled with the spirit of exploration as I set out on my solo trip. I'd never left the country before (outside of visiting Israel in high school with my church group and missionary trips to Central America), and I was thrilled.

I also looked forward to partaking in my first openly gay relationship. Months before leaving, I'd set my geographic filters on a dating app to Rome, hoping to match with someone I could experience Europe. I matched with a guy studying abroad in Rome, and we made plans to meet up.

The day we were to meet, I went on a tour of the Vatican. We planned to meet in the square just outside the basilica, and it was love at first sight; we both felt the electric pulse of passion running through our veins. It felt like being with Jake, except this time, there was no secrecy. We toured the countryside, spending an enchanting weekend together in Cinque Terre. We made passionate love that weekend and fell hard for each other.

I decided I wanted him in Paris with me, so I flew him up for the weekend, and we explored the city and each other. It was one of the most magical experiences of my life. Despite the paralyzing fear of going to hell, I decided from that point on that I was no longer going to settle for hiding my true nature. So I set out to discover who I am.

Cynics and Critics

The critics surfaced as they learned about my new way of life. One in particular, a man I hadn't spoken to since I was in high school, reached out via Facebook Messenger. He said he'd learned about the errors of my ways and quoted the scripture I'd relentlessly studied: "men did shameful things with other men, and as a result of this sin, they suffered within themselves the penalty they deserved."

My reply: "Yep, looks like I'm going to hell, then." After expressing his condolences, I gave him a tip on how to be a minister. Consequently, I lost the follows of both his children after I posted his message on Instagram. There were other trolls along the way, but few so blatant to give me the freedom to tell them to go to hell.

I started to feel the conditional nature of love in the Christian community. As long as I abided by specific rules, I was safe and accepted. Unfortunately, I needed to follow this code to stay in the group, or else I was out. It made me wonder if I was ever really loved by anyone in the church or whether it was solely what I had to offer to the faith that gained me acceptance. Hurt and confused, I wondered if my community in the church was nothing but a lie. I desired more than anything to belong somewhere, and it was becoming clear to me that belonging in the church was conditional.

Ultimately, the fear of losing my community was the one thing that kept me holding on. After leaving the church, I realized that their community was nothing but a bunch of insecure, conditionally loving humans, so losing them became more palatable. The fear of losing myself became more significant than the fear of losing my "friends." It was all I knew, and it no longer fit.

I maintained only a few of the many relationships I had in the church. Some of those have become close friends and great examples of Jesus' love. In essence, I had to learn what community meant to me and build my own tribe.

Heartbroken

The relationship with my European lover failed shortly after I moved to Los Angeles, and he moved back to New York. We talked about building a life together – getting married and having kids. It felt strange to talk about this after knowing each other for only a few months, but it also felt right. I was in a love relationship that was mutual with a man for the first time in my life. I couldn't imagine a life without him … until things ended.

It was a tragic breakup that I initiated after he lied to me on multiple occasions. By the end, we were utterly repulsed by the idea of one another. We shared a harsh exchange full of piercing words and called a stop to it. The final knife to the heart occurred while I was on vacation in Canada. After trying to make the relationship work for the third time, I learned about a romantic rendezvous he'd planned with an ex of his that he'd failed to share with me. I found out through social media that he had cheated on me, and it hurt more than anything I could ever have imagined. He kept trying to reach out to me, but I told him it was better he leave me alone or I would out him to his father for being gay, who had reached out to me over social media, wondering when I'd revisit their family. After exchanging hurtful words, I blocked him and moved on.

A New Perspective

New to Los Angeles and with only a handful of family members in the area, I set out to build a community of my own. I wasn't sure where to start, so I plugged into the LGBT affinity group through work. I was introduced to the group during an ice cream social they were having for Pride Week. I didn't know what to expect, so I asked my co-workers if they would join me. Once introduced to some of the members, I knew I'd found my people.

I quickly became involved with the organization; I volunteered for different events and met great people along the way. My enthusiasm caught the attention of the regional leader, who eventually asked another guy and me to co-lead the LA chapter. I was thrilled by the offer and immediately accepted. We grew the organization's activities to more than 40 events a year, almost one per week. I was having a blast exercising skills I'd picked up as an outreach pastor. I was building my new community, and it felt amazing.

However, throughout a couple of years, I came to a sobering realization: What I was doing in my new gay community was no different than my pursuits in the Christian community. I found myself in a familiar rut of depression, anxiety, comparison, and lackluster energy. What had once felt like reclaiming ground became another experience of lost identity. Just as I had done with the church, I tried different personalities to fit in and be accepted by my new community. I wanted someone or something to give me meaning — to define who I was and what I wanted. I was hungry for anything that would provide me with purpose, to be told how to act or who to be because I didn't know who I was.

I didn't find my groove until I stopped doing the stereotypical gay activities I thought I needed to prove my sexuality. I pulled away from the West Hollywood parties, Sunday brunches, gay activism, and drag shows. These activities weren't destructive like the church community, but my motives needed recalibrating. I was striving once again to put on identities to find acceptance and belonging.

Regardless of whether it was the church or the secular world, my motives were to fit in, and I thought this was what I needed to do to be accepted. This coping mechanism was learned in the church and used as a blueprint for forming other communities. But ultimately, I was still running away from myself. It wasn't until a series of failed relationships that I came to a great awakening about this and decided to get some help.

GETTING HELP

Onward and Upward

I eventually decided that the Christian faith altogether no longer fit me. For a few years after officially renouncing my faith, I was constantly awakened from night terrors about going to hell when I died because I was pursuing the *sin* of homosexuality.

The most common terrors hit eerily too close to home. A dream I remember vividly was set in the sanctuary at Bayside. I felt the searing eyes branding my soul as I walked through the doors. These were the most devout church members who judged me with their Christian niceties. I knew the moment I turned my back that they were going to talk shit about me in the form of a "prayer request" and feeling so self-conscious about it. In the dream, I heard some of the gossips painted in Christian terminology.

Their demeanor in the dream was very much like how I had been taught to treat wayward Christians by "being an example of Jesus' love to the lost." I remembered phrases like, "You may be the only Bible anyone ever reads," and feeling guilty for being a "false teacher who was destined for hell for leading other believers astray" since I was now pursuing my homosexuality. Nevertheless, I knew I was their project, that they had some sort of mystical charm to bring "the wayward sheep back into the fold."

Next I knew, the dream went dark. This darkness was more than just a memory; I felt it viscerally. The darkness ravished my soul, making me feel hollowed out. There also appeared to be a visual description of hell that my bible college teacher once taught: a "worm that never dies." This worm was nestled in my stomach, having its way with my inners. I thought this was my hell for choosing homosexuality over God. I almost always woke up frantically from these terrors drenched in sweat and tears. The voices of their indoctrination filled my mind, wondering if I had made the right choice to leave the faith.

Experimental Homosexuality

I was keenly aware that I needed to form a new community. While conditional, I had created around me a tribe of people who had my back when the going got tough. I knew there were certain friends I could call on to help me with specific struggles in life. Moving to Los Angeles was good in many ways, but it was also brutally revealing just how alone and unaware I was.

After the failed European romance, I picked up the pieces and took the lessons I thought were applicable. Then, when I had a panic attack from the traumas of my loss and the move to a city where I had nobody to turn to, I chalked it up to my vices. I thought I'd given over to the lusts of my sexuality, and what I desired was something more intimate - something more substantial. So I decided to date around a bit to see what I needed.

New to the city with only family members to call upon, I found myself going to bars, sitting alone at the counter, and chatting with bartenders. I'd initially adopted this practice when I'd moved back home since I was both comfortable being alone but also wanted some camaraderie. It proved to be a worthy tradition as I found my best friend after frequenting my favorite Los Angeles downtown bar.

We lost connection for three years but reunited at a mutual friend's concert and have been inseparable ever since.

One night, this habit led me to a nightclub where I met the gaze of one specific guy. We exchanged niceties, and I eventually decided to take him home. The following day, we exchanged numbers, and I asked him on a date.

My relationship with Tom was the first long-term relationship I ever had with a man — if you can call eight months long-term. As our relationship unraveled, I became more aware of what I wanted in a partner. It wasn't that Tom was lacking, but he didn't offer what I truly needed. His physical attributes were the sole reason I pursued him first, and as I got to know him, I knew something didn't fit.

I thought my priority was simply how a man looked, but as I continued in this relationship, depth became more attractive (and more of a focus). I learned that I strongly desired someone with whom I could connect on a spiritual level. The only problem? I didn't know what spiritual meant to me anymore.

Self-Hater

At this point in my journey, I was on my way to embracing more than just my sexuality; I was embracing myself. I

MY GAY CHURCH DAYS

was getting my bearings in the gay community, dating, and enjoying the company of men. What was once experienced as an "abomination" became an absolute joy. I was learning what it was like to date men and appreciate them for who they were. Yet, while learning about them, I was also learning who I was for the first time.

I constantly found myself lost in the magnificence of men, not conscious that I was discovering myself simultaneously. I frequently took on the identity of men I saw; on dates, I'd think about what I found most compelling about the man I was with and transform parts of myself to fit that. If he was interested in spirituality, I sought out crystals and gems. If he was interested in nature, I plucked up the courage to one day join him on a camping trip (a campsite, to me, is simply a hotel without amenities). If he was into fitness, I attended the same fitness cult he was involved with (aka any fitness craze in Los Angeles). Regardless of the guy, I somehow found a way to relate to him and discover something new about myself.

But there was one whose character was too much for me to handle...because it hit way too close to home.

One of my best friends was dating a member of the Los Angeles Gay Man's Chorus. He'd found this love over the holidays, so it was my duty (along with another of my best friends) to show our support by attending the Chorus' annual holiday event. As stunning as the performance was, it was nothing compared to the man with whom I locked eyes — I couldn't help but crush on him. When he met my gaze, though, I did the sudden look-away out of shyness.

Eye contact comes easy for me in conversation — meeting someone's eyes shows engagement and interest, and I always want to offer such manners. But meeting the gaze of a stranger horrifies me, even to this day! I once had a roommate who could've taught a master class on how to lock eyes with a stranger wherever, whoever. Not me. This widely insecure, newly-out homosexual found it even hard to make eye contact when I was buzzed at a bar, let alone with a stranger at some fancy event. But for whatever reason, this time was different.

To break the uncomfortable streak of intense staring, I made a move to introduce myself. He was just as charming as he looked, with a devilish smile and eyes that could melt metal. This was one of few encounters with this caliber of a man — what I wouldn't do to be his! We chatted a bit, exchanged numbers, and decided to know each other on a first date. I couldn't wait.

We decided to meet up for an afternoon coffee at my favorite cafe at the time. I arrived first, and I was so nervous I couldn't stay focused. Although we'd been texting intimate things to each other, I was terrified of our first "real" date. I ordered coffee and headed to the high-top area where I knew I'd feel most comfortable. When he walked in, my heart started pounding. He was even more gorgeous than I'd remembered, especially in his casual attire. We'd met dressed in our best, and yet somehow, he couldn't have looked better in that coffee shop.

We first dabbled in small talk — asking about holiday plans and what we were most excited about. Then, as was fitting for the season, the conversation shifted into a discussion about religion. Little did I know that this little texting flirt was a devout Christian. OK, I thought, this is not unfamiliar territory. Sure, it would've been weird for him to break that ice over text, but I wasn't expecting this from our sexy texts. Although it had been years since I'd set foot in a church, my Christian faith wasn't far removed. I still respected the teachings of Jesus but heavily condemned any form of Christian formalities. Curious, I obliged in our conversation.

He began telling me about the depth of his faith. His explanation was child's play in the sandbox of Christianity for me as he made blanket statements that included trigger words. Eventually, the truth came out, as I requested elaboration on terms I knew were code for much more radical and militant beliefs — so extreme that he revealed an abyss of self-hate in explaining them. It was the same self-hating rhetoric that once told me the essence of me was dirty and rotten. That said, "men did shameful things with other men, and as a result of this sin, they suffered within themselves the penalty they deserved." (Romans 1:27) A belief system that gave me nightmares for years. All these things were his manifesto.

If someone had thrown ice water on me at that moment, it would have instantly evaporated. My blood started to boil as a rage emerged that was so righteous and zealous it could have lifted a car. All this time, I'd been finding my identity in other men, and here I was brought to life by the assault of a former identity.

He quoted easy and cheap Christian clichés like, "homosexuality is an abomination before God" and "God weeps at the sight of gay parades." I wasn't surprised by this admission; after all, the church's most common narrative regarding "Gay Pride" is to push the "gay agenda." I once believed these lies, telling myself that gay people were celebrating evil and sin. It wasn't until I did my own research on gay history that I realized the importance of LGBTQ Pride. Our founding fathers in the LGBTQ community set forth to achieve equal treatment under the law. It was a crusade for Civil Rights, birthed out of much pain and torcher after the horrific police raid on the Stonewall Inn.

Not only were gays not protected under federal law, but wildly discriminated against by anti-gay legislation. LGBTQ Pride, I learned, was not an act of demanding *special rights* but demanding *equal rights*. Instead, pride in our community is an act of expressing freedom to celebrate our sexuality to normalize LGBTQ culture after hundreds of years

of discrimination in the United States and negative stereo-
types by the media. Pride is an expression of *equality* and
belonging.

Back in the coffee shop, I implored him to exercise his
militant beliefs with proof: "Tell me, where does the Bible
say that homosexuality is a sin?" He looked like a deer
caught in headlights. After admitting he couldn't furnish a
single verse because he didn't know the Bible well, he proceeded to say that he felt that this was what God ordained.
I lost my shit.

After giving him a lesson on Biblical studies and label-
ing his beliefs complete bullshit, the attention of the entire room was upon us. I could feel the eyes of others on
us, wondering about the strange couple at the high table.
There I was, unable to control the pitch of my voice, school-
ing this amateur in his own game. I felt pity and anger
towards him, at the same time an immense sense of defen-
siveness. Although it wasn't evident to me at the time (as I
defended ground I had gained from a former loss of faith),
this man was projecting his self-hate.

Clearly, this man was afflicted by his belief system that
said his sexuality was a curse. His homosexuality was a
burden too heavy to bear, and a religious system that consumed the feeble-minded was more than willing to indoc-
trinate him. He had internalized church talking points and
found shame in the very things about himself that at-

tracted him to men. These talking points were only too familiar to me. This man hated himself so much that he was
willing to be spiritually tortured for it.

Years after this explosive date, my housemate and I ran
into him. My housemate knew him well and filled me in
on some confidential information about him. Having this
knowledge and perspective, my pity turned to empathy. I
learned that day that people act out in ways that demon-
strate how they view themselves. It was a projection of his
own shame and humiliation, and to find some sort of reprieve and meaning, he turned to an antiquated system of
belief that brought deliverance from this shame.

Sound familiar?

Sean

I dated a fair number of men after Tom, falling in love
with some and lusting over others. But nothing was like the
love I felt with Sean.

Our first encounter was serendipitous — we met at his
birthday party. I was told we'd be a great match beforehand
but didn't take the comment to heart. At the time, my
mother was suffering from some health issues, so most of
my attention was focused on her. Therefore, Sean hit me

like a freight train. I was told, "You find someone when you least expect it, when you aren't looking for anyone." We hit it off instantly, so powerfully I feared setting fire to the place with the sparks between us.

Within hours we'd exchanged numbers and planned to meet in the coming week. Our first date felt like a scene from a movie: dinner and a cuddle make-out session on the beach, under the stars. I'd never felt so close to anyone in my life, and I barely knew him. We continued this way, texting each other love messages and finding time to be with each other every chance we got. But after just under a month of dating, things took a turn for the worse, and I slumped into a massive depression.

As quickly as it had started, it ended. The signs in my body were the first warning, as my inability to perform in the bedroom became more profound. His shots over the bow were his ever-more-pronounced distance — he lacked enthusiasm around our weekend romances. I was at a loss; how could something that had started so powerfully and beautifully be reduced to such indifference and formality?

As was the custom, I looked within and went on the attack. What had I done to destroy this romance? Was I too clingy? (He had been, too.) Did I give him too much attention? (It was mutual.) Was I not attractive enough? (He had his flaws.) The truth was I'd felt unworthy of this love from the start, and his careless actions reinforced those feelings.

Desperate for answers, I texted Sean to get an explanation, only to be met with absolute silence. I sought anything to stop the voices in my head from telling me what an absolute piece of shit I was, that I was unworthy of being loved. Finally, I resolved that it had been all my fault, just as I had with Jake. He was avoidant, and I could feel it. When a phone call ended it all, I was devastated. I knew I needed to get help, or things would not end well for me. I immediately called a therapist, who referred me to someone in my healthcare plan network. I didn't care, just as long as they could deal with an ex-Evangelical Christian pastor who was now openly gay.

Dr. Rachael

I was sitting in Dr. Rachael's waiting room when I got Sean's text in response to my request to talk things out in person. He was even colder than the lead-up to our breakup, and I didn't know how to respond. Once called into Dr. Rachael's office, she could tell by the look on my face that I was in shock. I told her about my romance with Sean, ending with why I was there and needed help responding to this text. She was gracious and helped me put into words how I was feeling. I sent the final text: "I understand this is what you need, but this is what I need" – words I'd never uttered or felt before. What was it like to "need" something – to vocalize what *I* needed? This was the last time I ever heard from Sean, just as a new chapter began with Dr. Rachael.

My past experiences with therapists had been bleak. I'd only seen the conversion therapist for a short while before I thought I could handle my sexuality myself. I'd also sought out a therapist between leaving the church and leaving the faith. She was a well-intentioned Christian therapist who helped me identify how I was feeling, but still within the context of "healing" my homosexuality. Therapy, therefore, hadn't been great, and I wasn't wildly optimistic about the prospects.

Things were instantly different with Dr. Rachael. She not only heard me but listened with compassion. Attentive to what I said, she had me put words to how I felt. The church's programming had been vast and deep, and she was willing to go to those depths with me. She understood the worldview I'd chosen to leave and the paralyzing loss of that community. She was able to explain my motives (that I'd been led to believe were sinful or evil) and identify the theme that I'd come to learn was all I ever wanted in life: to belong.

Belong. It was a word I hadn't thought of much, but it provoked a flurry of emotions when discussed in therapy sessions. I realized everything I'd done, everything I'd created, everything I'd become stemmed from a deep-seated desire to *belong*. I'd compromised and forsaken my values to belong in the church. I'd chosen to submit to ridiculous requests because I just wanted to belong. I'd feared going to hell, being separated from my community if I partook in sinful acts like homosexuality. What she helped me come to see was that I never really belonged to myself.

I hated myself. I couldn't look in the mirror without thinking about what a wretched sinner I was. I was disgusted with myself. But Dr. Rachael helped me dig out of my self-deprecation and bring truths I had stuffed away into subconsciousness. She let me open up, and I trusted her more and more as she showed loving compassion for my situation. Where I once was guarded, she allowed me to reveal some things about myself I wanted to hide.

She suffered right alongside me as I brought up the Sean experience for over a year. Rather than talk about him, she guided me to deeply explore the emotions I was feeling at the time and sit with them without judgment. This process helped me identify my triggers and why they were triggers to begin with.

I learned that the concept of salvation had become my greatest trigger. It was a prevalent and pervasive theme in my life. I once believed that Jesus could save me — that he would be the center of my affection and attention. If I denied his salvation, I'd be sent to hell, separated from everyone I knew and loved. I thought I could save others and become the center of their affection and attention at some point in my life. The belief that anyone needed saving implied that they weren't whole and that someone else could fill in the gaps. Where Jesus once promised this to me, I promised it to others.

What I actually needed was to save myself — to be my own center of affection and attention. I was looking for it from everyone but me. My feelings of inadequacy were a result of me not belonging to myself. Whenever a relationship ended, it was the most devastating thing that could happen because I thought what I needed was outside...when it was within the whole time.

Leaving Before Being Left

In therapy, we also addressed my excessive need to give. I tended to lean in hard in relationships — for example, offering money to help whoever I was dating at the time. I paid for everything (hotel, travel, food) for my European romance. I often picked up the bill on expensive nights out. I offered to pay for repairs on someone's car. I felt I had the resources to be a provider, which pleased me to be of service. What I thought I lacked in certain areas I could make up for with monetary provisions.

This wasn't exclusive to romantic relationships, either. I constantly found myself bearing the burden of the bill with friends. I didn't have the voice to speak up for myself and let others treat me rather than always treat them. For example, my friends and I once went out to celebrate in West Hollywood after a successful event with the LGBTQ group from work. One friend said she'd buy us bottle service. But when the night was over, I was left with the bill. The next day, the friend asked me how much it was. I felt terrible telling her the entire cost, so I only told her half the amount. I felt like I needed to provide for my friends that night. So, I brought it upon myself.

I wanted badly to belong, and being a provider was my way of belonging. Dr. Rachael helped me come to this realization, knowing this wasn't a healthy or prosperous way to keep friends. She constantly gave me ways to think about money, giving me practical exercises to help unlearn destructive beliefs.

I learned that giving was my way of ascribing value to myself. I thought so poorly of myself that I needed to "prove" my worthiness of love. Offering gave me some sort of meaning — a purpose in relationships. And it was a one-way street: I didn't want anything back because then I'd feel I owed the other person something. I tried to deflect. As much as I gave the impression of being selfless, I was being very selfish.

I needed to learn how to be vulnerable and receive. Receiving was vulnerable for me because it left me in a place of discomfort. I didn't know how to respond to someone's kindness, especially in a love relationship. Since I thought I was unworthy of love, I found purpose in giving. Unfortunately, this became a self-indulging act, as it kept the other person at arm's length. As long as I didn't have to be vulnerable, I was the one in control and could pull the trigger if threatened.

I sometimes pulled the trigger first if I felt I was eventually going to be left. I wanted to beat them to the punch, to soften the blow. That is why Sean leaving first hit so hard – I didn't see it coming. I didn't want to be dumped because it would mean, yet again, rejection. If someone left me, I'd be by myself and would be forced to sit with how I'd fucked it up. I needed a distraction — someone else to distract me from having to work on myself. I feared getting to know who I was because, for a long time, I was running away from him—suppressing him—holding him back. Being myself scared me.

Tools

Little by little, I'm now learning to have loving compassion for myself. Therapy has given me tools to help me do this. In our work together, Dr. Rachael rarely offered advice;

instead, she posed questions to help me come to my own answers. What she taught me was that I have the answers; I just need to trust myself more. I needed to have more compassion for myself, more empathy, and step into my world to see my perspective (just as I do for friends).

I went through several phases in my exploration of self. The men I dated became blueprints — they showed me glimmers of their identities that I found attractive. To please them, I took an interest in those things. Throughout those relationships and the help of therapy, I was then able to see that what I found most attractive in those men was actually what was most attractive in *me*. I wasn't a copycat; I was just learning who I was and what I loved about myself.

Victoria

I had a phase of what I called *Los Angeles spirituality* after the whole "what's-his-name season" (Dr. Rachael and I agreed — after quite some time had passed and I'd gotten over Sean — that this was the term to use whenever it came back up in sessions. I've rarely used it since). This phase involved going to healers, buying crystals, participating in guided meditations, doing sound baths, going to spiritual conventions, you name it! Life seemed to swing like a pendulum. Where I'd once drunk the Kool-Aid of the church, I was now consuming the secular version. I read up on the healing properties of certain crystals and the power of energy forces and wore rose quartz around my neck to attract love. I was hungry for something so powerful and so fulfilling that I would pursue it at whatever cost.

After being introduced to a few spiritual healers from different sets of friends, I came to realize that what I was pursuing was no different than what I'd followed in the church. I was looking for other people to give me my power without realizing I had the power myself, and I just needed to trust it. I sometimes wonder if Dr. Rachael allowed me to go down this spiritual path to let me figure this out for myself, knowing I now had the tools not to be deceived like my past. She gave me hidden nuggets every week — sound advice that didn't seem applicable at the time but hit me days or sometimes weeks later.

My quest to find spiritual healers ended with Victoria. By this point, I'd been through the gambit of healers but thought I'd give this one a try since she was held in such high regard by two different sources. I showed up at her house, not knowing what I was getting myself into. She was a chakra healer, and to be completely honest, I had no idea what that meant. I soon realized that Victoria was the missing piece — someone just like me but who had the unique ability to feel into others' energy sources.

What made her the real deal was that she wasn't like the others, promising that if you followed a course or paid a crazy amount of money, you would one day arrive. It was a cycle of dependency — as you got more into the belief system, you became more dependent on the leaders as you realized your inadequacy. But Victoria was different: the first thing she ever said to me was that she would teach me how to tap into my own power and open up my energy sources on my own. She didn't want me dependent; she wanted me healed.

She was also prophetic. Without knowing a thing about me, in our first session, she said she saw a little boy sitting politely at the front of a church, in a pew, waiting for his commands. It couldn't have been a more accurate description of me and what I was going through at the time. Her sessions were filled with revelations like this, bringing both healing and understanding about who I was and what I was destined to create in my life.

When I explained why I felt shame over how I'd reacted to certain events when I was a child and teen, she helped me understand that I was just trying to protect myself. I was surviving and did it the way I found worked the best for me without any tools. As an adult, I've been given many tools – both for life and in terms of learning new tricks to help me defend against attacks and define who I am. I can take care of myself; I don't need to be anyone's savior. I don't need to be anyone's provider. I am perfect the way I am and deserve the same love I have to give.

For me, this was more than just personal. Victoria demonstrated that those in the secular world possessed the same gifts the church claimed exclusive rights. For example, in youth group, they taught that specific missionaries were "filled with the Spirit of God" and could heal infirmities simply by placing their hands on people. I knew a girl who swore that when she put her hands on a woman's tumor, she felt it vanish as she prayed over her. These stories haunted me. If they were true, it meant God was real and what he said in the Bible was true, which meant I was going to hell. But Victoria was a living embodiment of the secular version of this, which showed me that you didn't have to be Christian to help people heal with Spirit.

Victoria answered my most profound spiritual questions, giving me new light and a fondness for a kind of spirituality I'd always found mysterious. I'd always felt some sort of connection to a higher being, but after leaving the church, I thought I had to give up those desires. Victoria gave me new life in this space, allowing me to understand spirituality in the secular context. No longer was it just the church that had access to spiritual sources. Instead, it was accessible to anyone who felt connected to spiritual things, and I was ready and willing to accept it.

After an abusive experience in the church and some secular healers, this was music to my ears. Victoria didn't deplete me of financial resources by telling me she had an extraordinary power or secret message, and all I needed to do was buy her special healing potions, lotions, or teachings. She didn't claim to have exclusive rights to the truth like the church and many secular healers. She was just a normal human being who struggled with life the same as anyone else but could tap into her unique magic.

She was different and had an extraordinary gift that, to this day, I still seek out, even as she has become one of my closest friends.

Today

My experiences in life shaped my worldview. There are plenty of factors that contribute to the formation of our worldview – how we were raised, what resources are available to us, the influences in our lives: who we look up to, and even who we consider enemies. Not wanting to lose what I thought was the most important relationship to my survival, my fears ran the narrative and shaped my worldview. Wanting reprieve from my harassers, I sought the affections of my father. Not wanting to lose my father's love, I sought the acceptance of a belief system that provided a "cure" to my most profound insecurity. Thus, my story began with a worldview shaped by the circumstances I was raised in and the tools I lacked. Actual environmental forces were at work, an instinctual response to my desperate attempt to stay alive.

My parents loved me the best they could with the tools they were given. Information acquired in their formative years was used to guide their understanding of family and replicate a family dynamic based on the cultural values that raised them. There were plenty of times in my childhood that I wished I had different parents, wondering what it would be like to have an "American family" like many other kids in school. I would listen to their communication style, watch how their parents talked to them, and show them affection. I would covet their experience and resent my own. It took some time for me to accept my family situation and honor it for what it was and come to admire the beautiful parts.

Today, I look back on my formative years, no longer with resentment but with thankfulness. I had been through quite a bit to arrive at where I'm today and thankful for my new relationships with my family – both blood and chosen. My dad and I respect and love each other for who we are, even though we have significant differences. After coming out to him the day after the 2016 election, it paved the way for us to have a relationship of authenticity. I was open and honest with him about my sexuality because of the horrendous election results – how I was no longer seeking approval for my sexuality or hiding my true identity. Our relationship may not be perfect today, but I wouldn't trade it in for anything anymore.

While spending time with my family, I had a unique opportunity to share what was going on in my life. We sat around my uncle's living room table while the guys shot the shit about the current sports statistics. Wildly bored by the conversation, I took out my computer and started working on the manuscript of this book. As my aunt was sitting behind me, she inquired about what I was working on. I was shaking. I hadn't officially come out to my family at large. My aunt had heard rumors of my sexuality, but we never really discussed it. Building up the courage, I started to share my life and why I was writing this book. Eventually, the interest of the entire room shifted on me.

I prefaced with saying that my book may be offensive to some in the room and hear me out. Then, they asked me the title. Being too shy, I decided to instead pass around my computer to show them the front and back cover of the book. Insecurities began to well up inside of me as each person got a good look at it. As it got around to my dad, my heart began to pound harder. As my computer came back around, my uncle and aunt implored me to read the back cover. I could sense my dad's anxiety but was reminded of the whole purpose behind writing this book. If I were willing to expose my greatest insecurities to the world, it would stand to reason that that would include my family.

After reading the book description in a shaking voice, the room erupted with amazement and praise! I couldn't believe it! The compliments from my family were one of the most rewarding and comforting feelings, but the greatest compliment came from my dad. He said to me, "I'm proud of you for sharing your convictions and using your voice to help other people." A sensation flowed through my body by his words. I know that he disagrees with me, but his recognition of my accomplishments was enough. I no longer needed his approval or desired him to agree with me, but I appreciated his support.

Another example of if only more Christians were like him.

My brother and sister have become my closest friends – not only making a truce with my brother but coming to celebrate each other's differences. It wasn't until I could step out of my world of hurt to acknowledge the path he trailblazed for me. My own coming out much smoother because of his groundwork in my family. We knew how to push each other's buttons and allowed old triggers to propel our bitterness towards one another. Finally, during my thirtieth birthday, we had a wonderful experience that we refer to as our "becoming brothers for the first time" moment. I am proud to say my brother has become one of my closest confidants and friend to this day.

My sister has always been an inspiration to my love. I've finally come to meet her at the level of her commitment and to see her for the brilliance she emanates. She is a stark reminder of my greatest deception and the ultimate example of grace. As guilty as I was for how I treated her, her grace abounds as we have pressed on to a much more intimate and genuine relationship. My sister is truly my most favorite person on earth, and I cherish our time with each other.

Another sobering reminder of my life of deception was my experience with my cousin on my mom's side of the family. I never was close to my mom's family as they were much more traditional than my dad's side. But this cousin has always been a free thinker in the family. Being raised in a Catholic school, she questioned the premise of the faith in high school after attending a religious camp. She asked her Bible teachers difficult questions, then met with cliche Christian lingo to comb things over. She wasn't buying it. Being close to my brother and experiencing firsthand his difficulties living his truth as a gay man, she felt defensive of him. She also despised the content I pushed in opposition to my brother and his lifestyle.

We were social media friends at best, never substantially coming into contact with each other in person. After reading social media posts on my relentless assault on the gay community, she became defensive of my brother by taking his experience into perspective.

Shortly after coming out, my parents and brother came to visit my mom's sister in Los Angeles and asked me to meet them there. My cousin would be there as well, which was the first time I had seen her in years. I wasn't sure what to expect considering my new lifestyle and her strong personality. After exchanging niceties, she told me in a private conversation: "I'm skeptical of your motives. I need to tell you, I defriended you on Facebook because of your ardent support of anti-gay propaganda." This took me back a bit, but no surprise in knowing her personality. She didn't care what people thought - she was in defense of the truth. After explaining my departure from the faith and accepting my true identity, she cautiously embraced me.

To this day, she is one of the most authentic and loving family members. We make it a point to meet up every week to catch up on life. Her strength, generosity, and honesty are my greatest inspiration.

With the handful of Christians in my life today, I have come to love and appreciate authentic Christianity. While the teachings of Jesus have been forsaken by many in the Evangelical movement, it has thus not affected my ability to admire the work of Jesus and what he truly set out to accomplish. I've been able to discern a real Christian from a CINO (Christian in name only), which has given me a fondness for the faith. Although not following the faith myself (nor ever will again, I can promise you that), I can appreciate and practice the teachings of Jesus in the spirit of his supposed words.

The scars of my former experience have healed over: visible yet no longer painful.

I know my journey is far from over, but looking back on the ground I have covered, I am confident that it was well worth the journey.

IT IS FINISHED

Although unique, my story is not dissimilar to that of many in the church. As children, we look up to the adults in our lives to give us love, compassion, and meaning. When I was introduced to a group of adults that appeared to have my best interests in mind, it seemed to give me the power to overcome some of my most significant challenges in life at that time. I was picked on relentlessly for my weight and sexuality. What I could control I was able to grow out of (my weight), but the one thing I couldn't change was my homosexuality. It goes without saying that a group that gave an out to my greatest insecurity was the force that drew me in the deepest.

There were times in my faith that I felt like a lost cause — that I'd never be delivered from my infirmities. This kept the cycle of dependency and depression intact as I pressed in deeper and harder to find my identity in something greater than myself. Little did I know that the greatness I was seeking was in me all along and that I was running from it faster than a bat out of hell. I believed that who I was was an abomination to the group to whom I had devoted my identity. Their acceptance was more important to me than my own self-acceptance. These equally insecure humans claimed to know how to break the curse of humanity — deliverance from sin and evil. All I had to do was submit to a higher being; I did, not realizing I was actually submitting to an antiquated belief system.

It took a few tumbles and divine intervention to get me out of the grip of this cycle of codependency, but it was well worth the journey. Where I once despised my past, today, I look back on it with a sense of fondness and admiration for how far I've come and who I have become. Although not delivered (I've learned that this process is a constant), I have arrived at a place of accepting myself for who I am and admiring the brilliance of my unique design.

The battle of dismantling this belief system of my youth and early adulthood is far from over, but it has lost much of its sting. Today I find myself with a greater sense of self-acceptance and love, battling ugly thoughts only in my more vulnerable moments. With my newfound tools and confidence, dismantling old beliefs has become more attainable as I evolve into my beauty.

I now strive to catch self-critical thoughts and turn them into thoughts of fondness for my unique nature. I hold close to the people and things I love most and let go of those that no longer serve me. When I look in the mirror, I tell myself how good I look rather than identifying the most shameful and painful parts of my body – most of the time. When dates don't work out, I change the narrative of "I'm not lovable or need to change to become the person they desired" to "It wasn't meant to be." Instead, I find love in my beauty and grace in my imperfections.

Most notably, I have struggled with gastrointestinal issues, which at times have affected my ability to perform in the bedroom. When these issues arose a few years ago, my healers pointed out that this was my body telling me something in my life was not right — that I needed to listen to the cries of my body.

In one instance, this involved an attempt to cling to my career. I worked for one of the Big Four accounting firms when the issue started to rear its ugly head. After much discussion with my healers, it was evident that the source of the affliction was rooted in my identity as a career person. As mentioned earlier, I had never been without a job since age ten, which fueled my identity in my work. Each career failure sparked a barrage of self-beratement and self-deprecation. My worthiness was wrapped up in what I *did* rather than who I *was*. I found myself up at night, tormenting myself for messing up a project or telling myself I was stupid and unworthy of good things. My identity had transferred to my work, which brought about other types of demons. After coming to this realization, I decided enough was enough. My health and wellness were more important than my career trajectory, so I gave notice. I instantly found momentary relief from my physical ailments. I learned that my body was communicating that this needed to be released - that it no longer served me.

The lesson was ongoing as I decided to submerge myself back into the career that was causing me pain. I chose to work for a smaller firm, thinking this would be my relief. After a few more years of this, I recently decided to leave the public accounting industry altogether to start my own firm, bringing another wave of relief from my physical infirmities.

It defied logic — we were amid a global pandemic, and I was in an industry that was the safest of all. Yet real logic was taking a holistic approach to self-care by considering more than just the physical. My mental and emotional health were just as important (if not more so) as my physical needs, so leaving public accounting altogether was an easier decision to make. My evolution and growth made the lesson long learned but well worth the journey.

All this is to say: I've learned that life is not about arriving but self-discovery. Life is sourced in the discovery of our own evolution. Just as the universe is constantly expanding, so are we. As products of the Big Bang (God would be pissed if He heard me call his creation that! Oh well), we are faced with the reality of the ever-expanding universe.

Our beings are a product of this miraculous existence, which means we're constantly faced with challenges that require us to evolve. I strongly believe in the concept of "evolve or die," meaning that we have a constant choice to grow out of the old versions of ourselves and into newer versions. Like the pairs of shoes of a child, we grow out of certain things and into bigger things. This is true for experiences and people in our lives. Being keenly aware of what serves us and what no longer suits us is part of this evolution.

You can choose to stay in the smaller version of yourself, which will only bring about resentment and turmoil. I've been there for many years, finding escape through the afflictions of others and myself. When we don't evolve, we're actively choosing to stagnate and allow decay. If we aren't evolving, then we aren't expanding. As painful as evolution may be, it is not nearly as unbearable as being stagnant. We're a byproduct of stardust in a constantly evolving universe. Our nature is to regenerate continually. Just as old skin turns to dust, so too do things that no longer serve us, yet often we stay complacent for pseudo-securities, like momentary comfort or *community*. This comfort becomes restlessness and evolves into anxiety and depression. When we aren't open to change, our minds become closed off to the world. And when we're closed off, we're cut off from the love and acceptance of not only others, but ourselves.

One of the greatest quotes concerning love and evolution was by none other than the famous Christian writer C.S. Lewis. In his book on the Four Loves, he writes:

"To love at all is to be vulnerable. Love anything and your heart will be wrung and possibly broken. If you want to make sure of keeping it intact you must give it to no one, not even an animal. Wrap it carefully round with hobbies and little luxuries; avoid all entanglements. Lock it up safe in the casket or coffin of your selfishness. But in that casket, safe, dark, motionless, airless, it will change. It will not be broken; it will become unbreakable, impenetrable, irredeemable. To love is to be vulnerable."

To love yourself is to be vulnerable.

Christianity was one of those things I grew out of far sooner than I could admit. While it gave me the power to overcome my accusers in high school, its belief system then permeated every avenue of my life, creating a cycle of codependency that was hard to break. Yet as suffocating as it was, it brought about significant challenges in my life that formed me into the person I am today. It caused me to break free from one of the most oppressive experiences in my life and ultimately look at life through the lens of my beauty and perfect imperfections. It called me to a higher way of living — to honor the spirituality that yearns within me while giving me enough knowledge to call bullshit when I see it. It's also great to have the knowledge I've acquired when encountered by "believers," as I can challenge them to know their own scriptures before condemning another homosexual to damnation.

I look forward to the day when I transcend this life, knowing that the mystery of the afterlife I once feared has now become my most remarkable anticipation. I only wish the same for you, dear reader.